Identification Technologies

To establish a system for identifying our citizens in a democratic society may cost us a minor degree of personal freedom. Not to do so may cost us all of it.

DEANE L. HUXTABLE
State Registrar
Commonwealth of Virginia

Identification Technologies
COMPUTER, OPTICAL, AND CHEMICAL AIDS
TO PERSONAL I D

By

GEORGE H. WARFEL

Technical Consultant
Menlo Park, California

CHARLES C THOMAS · PUBLISHER
Springfield · Illinois · U.S.A.

109549

Published and Distributed Throughout the World by
CHARLES C THOMAS • PUBLISHER
Bannerstone House
301-327 East Lawrence Avenue, Springfield, Illinois, U.S.A.

© *1979, by* CHARLES C THOMAS • PUBLISHER
ISBN 0-398-03889-9
Library of Congress Catalog Card Number: 78-25619

Library of Congress Cataloging in Publication Data

Warfel, George H.
    Identification technologies.

    Bibliography: p.
    Includes index.
    1. Identification. I. Title.
HV8073.W354   364   78-25619
ISBN 0-398-03889-9

Printed in the United States of America
C-1

PREFACE

PERSONAL IDENTIFICATION is rapidly moving from an art, practiced by everyone, to a science, performed by computers. Of course, we will continue to recognize our friends (and our enemies) by chance glances and scraps of conversation overheard in a group situation. But proof of identity in a commercial sense will soon be the task of electronics, optics, and chemistry.

This trend is so new that it is difficult to forecast which way it will develop. The computer will undoubtedly influence the decision, but the data-gathering sensors of tomorrow's "ID machine" are probably still on the drawing board.

So that we might have a better insight into what is coming, the work of a few hundred engineers and scientists in the field has been gathered into this book. Most of the background came from seminars, classroom lectures, and conference papers of the past three years. The patents referenced are generally recent ones, and, no doubt, many more are still pending and bogged down in the procedures of the Patent Office.

In preparing this book, as with any new effort, the author was hampered by a lack of acknowledged terminology. In most cases, the problem was circumvented by using phrases or lifting words from other areas. In one instance, however, it was essential to establish a convenient, easily used term because it appears so frequently. This is the case of "the person being identified."

The term *identifyee* was selected as a fitting word. It is hoped it will become a part of the jargon in the expanding field of identification technology.

The thorough reader may also note that a few examples used in the earlier chapters are repeated later in the chapters devoted to specific techniques. This was done, in part, to reinforce the philosophies of identification as a permanent part of our present and future social environment. It was also done for the benefit of those whose narrow specialty might lead them to skip the first four chapters and read only the ones that bear on their field.

I hope those who read this volume as it was written, from front to back, will be forgiving.

GEORGE H. WARFEL

P.O. Box 627
Menlo Park, California

ACKNOWLEDGMENTS

I AM GRATEFUL to Dr. Noel M. Herbst of IBM, Willard F. Rockwell, III of Rockwell International, Dr. George R. Doddington of Texas Instruments, and Paul Meissner of the National Bureau of Standards, for their help with references and thoughts on the future.

Throughout the preparation of the manuscript, my greatest help came from my wife, Joann, a professional librarian. To her, and to her many colleagues in the university and corporate libraries across the country, go my heartfelt thanks.

G.H.W.

CONTENTS

ix

Identification Technologies

Chapter 1

PERSONAL IDENTIFICATION IN THE MODERN WORLD

A WIDESPREAD NEED for personal identification (ID) and the technology to provide it have been simultaneous with the second half of the twentieth century. Unfortunately, the need and the technology have both preceded social acceptance. Many people resent being identified by a machine or device, rather than by a person. Even more people prefer to remain completely anonymous. In addition, the criminal, living under an alias, is hostile toward any effort that tends to uncover his true identity.

NEED FOR IDENTIFICATION

The population today is mobile. A working person may be engaged by half a dozen different employers in the course of his working life and may have twice that many residences. The taxes on a residence today make it foolhardy for the average family to live in quarters that are larger than necessary. Thus, a young couple may start out in a modest home or apartment and then may move to a different neighborhood as the family increases. Soon, another move may be necessitated to reside in a preferred school district. As the family grows and the older children begin to leave home, another move may be necessary to acquire a smaller, less expensive residence. Each time, there are new neighbors, new merchants, different church and municipal officials, each requiring that the recent arrivals identify themselves. With each employment, a worker must also provide proof of identification. This may be a driver's license, references, or perhaps a résumé of previous schooling. All of these factors are recorded, and some will be checked out. At most large plants, new employees must submit to some degree of initial identification and than reidentify themselves each time they pass through the plant gates.

For those working in high-security areas, a higher level of identification is required both at the time of employment and upon entry into the inner complex. An employee may even be

3

deterred from starting on the job until his identity is proven. The United States government has established a system of "clearances" with a hierarchy of six ranked steps. Records are maintained for each person, both civilian and military, involved in handling classified matter. Persons who are on this roster must constantly identify themselves so that the government can monitor their activities. These people cannot relax their vigil and must not travel without identification on their person. To hold a secret or top secret clearance is not only something to be proud of, but it may also be essential to one's job.

In a typical plant of two thousand employees, the following ID plan would be executed daily:

New employee–computer complex
High-level security "clearance" applications are processed at the rate of five a day.

New employee–production
Thirty personal history ID records are processed each day.

Plant entry
Twenty-eight hundred badge-check IDs are performed at the entry gates.

Computer center entry
Four hundred fifty password IDs are performed each day.

Visitors
Twenty visitors' signatures are logged with time in and time out.

Such a plant would have a security force of twenty guards and a staff of at least three in the employment department, checking identification and issuing badges. Although such activity is costly and necessary, it does not improve the product or add to the profits.

The same person who is employed at this plant is required to identify himself in a totally different way when he returns to his apartment in the evening. As he enters the lobby, he must indicate to a machine or a person that he is authorized to enter. This involves still a lower level of ID, lower even than the plant entrance. The person entering the apartment lobby does not really state who he is, but only that he is a member of the group that is to be admitted. The apartment management may alter the ID techniques every two or three months to deter vandals or imposters, but usually a memorized, three-digit number suffices.

The person has to identify himself again if he goes out to supper and pays the bill with a credit card. Here, he is required to sign a paper, and the signature should match that on the card. This level of ID affirms that he is the person to whom the card was issued. Prior to receiving the card, he had to identify himself in some detail at his bank. He had to make statements as to where he lived and where he worked. The bank verified these statements by calling the apartment manager or checking the city directory and by calling the personnel department of the stated employer. Thus, the party is in a closed loop of many strands. If any one of the paths leads to an area of questionable truth, he will sacrifice some of the benefits of the society in which he lives. Yet, many try to "beat the system,"–and many succeed.

FREQUENT IDENTIFICATION IS A NEW CONCEPT

The reason that many people succeed in beating the system is that the North American society has not yet accepted the fact that frequent, almost constant ID is an essential facet of modern life. When our grandfathers lived and raised their families in the same house in which they were born, ID was not a critical item. Trust was granted on sight, and the local people all knew each other. In the frontier, it was generally assumed that most of the people were there because they had become involved in a problem in the more civilized parts of the country, and trust was seldom granted to new arrivals. Business and personal relationships relied on instant performance. A gun was more likely to get respect than a good credit record. Thus, ID was not important in either the frontier, where it was meaningless, or in the more established societies, where it was unnecessary. Today, however, there is no frontier, and due to the rapid movement of families across the country, one could almost say that there is no "established" society. Hence, ID has become a necessity at the place of residence, at the place of employment, and wherever a person does business. These alone require that a person be identified three or four times a day.

The most frequent use of identification arises in the financial transaction area. While checks are a part of this, credit transactions are the dominant volume. When a check is mailed to pay a bill, ID is not required. It is unlikely that some imposter is fraudulently paying another person's bills. When a check is offered for merchandise that is to be taken from the store, the merchant asks for identification, because he wants to be sure that the document is valid before he delivers the merchandise. In the case of using a monthly revolving account, such as a charge account at a department store, the ability of the customer to pay has been previously established. In this case, ID may be requested, as with the check, when the goods are delivered, but not when the bill is paid. For such purposes, ID usually means presenting a plastic card, previously issued by the store and bearing the customer's signature. Generally, the custom is that mere possession of the card identifies the customer. Seldom are the signatures compared.

Where ID becomes involved with a check is when the check is presented for cash. The teller or clerk must be sure that the maker is the proper person. Once cash is given for a forged check, it is almost impossible to backtrack and recover the money. To prosecute is expensive and may only land the forger in jail. While this stops others from being victimized by the forger, it does not improve the balance sheet.

TODAY'S ID METHODS

The average United States citizen carries many documents of identification in his possession at all times. While each document may be different, they all relate to the person.

Check-cashing Cards

Many banks have issued what are called *courtesy cards* for check cashing. By any other name, they are ID cards. Usually the cards are simply paper stock, with a bank logo and some computerized printing on them and a blank for a signature. The cards are issued to those of known financial backing and are merely proof of a sound bank relationship. The signature is the ID. The card conveys the right to cash a check (usually up to one hundred dollars) at any branch of the bank. Of course, the bank is the one where the person has an account. In states where branch banking exists, this is a distinct advantage to the customer of a sprawling branch bank. Such cards have little meaning in unit banking states, such as Illinois or Texas. So far, courtesy cards or check-cashing cards have not been issued for interbank use.

Gasoline Credit Cards

The gasoline credit card provides a unique situation in transaction ID. It is well known that the automobile is the most controlled piece of portable property that a person can own. It is registered to the owner and to his loaner (if the owner has not paid for it totally), and it bears a metal license plate. This license is related to the above-mentioned owners and to the serial numbers put on the engine and frame when the car was manufactured. Each state maintains a large, computerized file of all of this data. Each sale or transfer must be registered with the state, along with the verification of all of the other numbers. Few people have rebelled at this intricate detail of identification, because it has evolved slowly and because it covers a machine, but it is the most complete identification of an object in the legal world today. If a human being were covered with as much identification, there would be howls of outrage.

It is detailed auto identification that allows the gasoline credit card to survive with a rather low record of fraud. Each purchase of motor fuel or an accessory for a motor vehicle has the license number of the involved vehicle recorded on the sale ticket. This record, and because the average sale is under ten dollars, tends to keep the fraud to a minimum. With the audit trail to the vehicle complete and the usual dollar amount low, the criminal considers the risk too great for the returns. This is a modern case of ID succeeding in preventing crime. Regrettably, the success has to be credited to a machine and a computer system, not to human honesty.

Bank Credit Cards

Central to the retail credit card business is the bank credit card. The annual dollar volume of bank cards is over 40 billion dollars. Because of the wide ranging marketing policies of bank cards, they have a fraud loss of over 50 million dollars per year.[1] The use of a bank card involves an agency or third-party relationship. First, a bank issues cards to thousands of customers. Then, a bank (perhaps–most likely–a different bank) signs agreements with hundreds of merchants. Then, one of the customers and one of the merchants join in a credit transaction for merchandise. Often, the transaction takes place far remote from the banks and while the banks are closed. It is the merchant who must ensure that the card is in the hands of the proper person. Yet, the bank has guaranteed the merchant that he will be paid for any purchase up to a certain limit (usually fifty dollars). The only requirement the bank places on the merchant is that he makes a reasonable effort to identify the customer as the proper cardholder. This usually means comparing signatures. In some instances, the card may carry a photo of the person to whom the card was issued. In these cases, the merchant or clerk endeavors to match appearances.

Identification, then, often poorly performed or not performed at all, is the only control on run-away fraud. Even this was forced on the banks. During the mid-1960s, when bank cards were beginning to be used, many cards did not have any means of ID. Not until the Federal Reserve, the regulatory board for national banks, established a regulation[2] did the banks take ID seriously. The enactment of a law has not done the job, however. It takes skill to match signatures, especially when they are crammed into small, square signature boxes. To match photographs requires that the parties involved look at each other squarely. Many people find this embarrassing. To many people, the performing of good ID is tantamount to a challenge, and to a retail sales merchant, this is contrary to his ingrained manner of treating his customers. Until an impersonal machine or device can perform the ID, the bank card will continue to have a high fraud rate.

Driver's License

The above examples cite frequent use of ID, but with rather an elite group, i.e. those people who have jobs and homes and who are creditworthy. There is a much larger group who carry ID; those with driver's licenses. It has been said that the driver's license is in the United States what the passport is in Europe.

The driver's license is the most accepted document of identification today. It is also a symbol of adulthood. Who has not seen a young person in ecstasy over receiving his driver's license? It is equivalent to the ancient tribal rites indicating the privilege to marriage. If you have ever known a young person who has failed the driver's test, you have known one in the deepest of despair. This coupon, this ticket, this simple document bearing a photo, physical description, and date of birth is the key to adulthood. It is also ID. With it, the legitimate holder has credibility. Without it, he is a nonperson.

Nondriver's License

There are older people who have failed the driving test. They thus become dependent on public bus services, private (and expensive) taxi services, and personal friends and family for transportation. They are not, however, deprived of ID. Almost every state provides for nondriver's licenses. These have all of the detail of a driver's license but do not confer the right to operate a vehicle. Some states even provide such documents for younger people who have been deprived of the right to drive temporarily. In the United States the driver's license has a dual function: (1) The original purpose, as a permit to operate a vehicle; and (2) to identify the holder. Recently, the secondary purpose has become the more important.

The extreme value placed on the driver's license as an ID document has led to a considerable traffic in false licenses. In fact, as the importance of an ID document has forced its way to the front, all forms of ID cards have become the target of counterfeiters. One can buy fraudulent credit cards, false birth certificates, driver's licenses, or employee pass cards–for a price, any kind of ID document is available.

FALSE IDENTIFICATION IS WIDESPREAD

In November, 1976, the Federal Advisory Committee on False Identification issued an eight-hundred-page report on false ID.[3] This committee, under the Department of Justice, produced a frightening amount of evidence that false ID, aliases, and cheating in business were a way of life to thousands of people. Cheating the government is apparently considered a proper sport, much as poaching was during the 1700s. There may be a similar feeling among the cheaters; that those with power are not deserving of that power and are not capable of protecting it–or even properly using it. It could be that there is a mild revolution, evidenced by widespread bilking of the government, and the principal weapon is false ID. If there is a revolt to quell, the first step is proper and adequate ID. The second effort, of course, should be to cure the cause, but arms must be surrendered and those involved must come to the negotiating table. We must have personal identification that is acceptable to all parties and sufficiently accurate to defy the cheaters.

The large-scale ID that has suffered the most abuse is in the welfare check crisis. In New York alone, cheating on welfare, both with checks and food stamps, was costing over one million dollars a year. While some of this was money given to people who, while properly identified, were undeserving of welfare, almost all of it involved false identification. Sometimes, the false ID occurred at the time of application, and sometimes it occurred via a forgery of stolen checks. The Welfare Department then cut the losses from fraudulent pickup of checks to less than $100,000 per year by issuing photo ID cards to the recipients.[4] The total loss to the United States taxpayer as a result of fraud in welfare systems is estimated at hundreds of millions of dollars annually.[5]

There are those who resent being identified. And, as noted above, losses do not go to zero with ID, nor is the ID method without its expenses.

The most complex ID method yet put into practice for a large group is the Alien Identification Card. This new card is being issued today to replace the 5 million Alien Registration Receipt cards now in circulation.[6] The card carries a photo, signature, fingerprint, and an encrypted ID code. This code contains certain numeric elements of all of the graphical components in its input data. This highly sophisticated card minimizes counterfeiting, which has been a problem for the Immigration and Naturalization Service for many years.

ANONYMITY AS A RIGHT

There could be good ID if the vociferous few who oppose it were willing to yield. Many think it is their right to remain anonymous, yet, they want to cash checks, drive cars, and use all of the government services, without saying who they are or where they live. These people, though a minority, feel that to ask who they are is an invasion of their privacy. They fail to realize that privacy, as an ideal, has been forced to change in the past two hundred years.

We can no longer expect to escape a bad career and move on to another town and start again. Upon arrival in the other town, we will be asked to identify ourselves, and if the previous escapade was too damaging, we will be returned to face the charges. If the identification system has performed its function, this is exactly what will happen. To refuse to be identified may still be considered a right, but the party is suspect. Within a few years, it may cease to be thought of as a right, and, a generation later, constant identification will be an accepted thing. There will be less crime when that day comes.

REFERENCES

1. Nilson, H. S.: Bankcard fraud will reach an all-time high of seventy-seven million in 1978. *Nilson Report.* Issue no. 161, Apr., 1977.
2. Board of Governors of the Federal Reserve System: Regulation Z, Sec. 226.13(c). (Truth in Lending Act, Sec. 133, effective Jan., 1972.)
3. Federal Advisory Committee on False Identification: *The Criminal Use of False Identification.* Washington, D. C., U. S. Dept. of Justice, 1976.
4. Santaguida, F.: Safeguarding unemployment payments. *Security World, 15(1):*1978.
5. McNally, J. P.: *Welfare Fraud and the Document Examiner.* Read before the Thirtieth Annual Meeting of the American Academy of Forensic Sciences, St. Louis, Feb., 1978.
6. New fraud-proof alien identification card. *Federal Law Enforcement Bulletin, 16(7):*1977.

Chapter 2

HISTORY OF PERSONAL IDENTIFICATION

W HEN ONE CONSIDERS the importance of personal identification in everyday life, it is surprising how slowly the techniques have developed. Even today, when the need for good identification methods is so obvious and the technology exists, there are strong forces opposing the application of ID systems. Many people fear that the widespread use of ID methods will interfere with their privacy, while others oppose it because it resembles totalitarianism.

BUSINESS OR TRANSACTION IDENTIFICATION

Although businesses have used ID methods in transactions for centuries, the use of sophisticated devices is recent. Years ago, the business community was a small, select group, known to each other by sight, and for most business this was the only ID. For transactions involving parties not known to each other, a third party knowing both other parties would vouch for their identities. For transactions involving distances or agency assignment, frequently artifacts, such as matching sticks or unique and readily identified stones, were used to identify a person representing someone else's interest. The signature was used only as a means of commitment–a means of acknowledging a promise. It was not thought of as an identification. As more people became capable of signing and as paper documents became more prevalent, the signature became not only the binder in a transaction, but also a means of identification. Many businessmen developed unique signatures, with flourishes and sweeping underlines, making their signatures unique as a means of identification. Certainly, these ornaments did not make the signed document any more binding, but it did make it easier to quickly recognize the maker, even though he was absent. As more of the general population became literate, paper documents began to multiply, and the signature became the popular method of ID and commitment in business transactions for the public.

The usual method of carrying out a signature ID is first to have a specimen signature on file. This specimen must be made at a time that someone in authority is present to identify the signer by positive means (a personal acquaintance with the signer or a group of two or three previously signed documents). With the file signature as a reference, documents can then be accepted by comparing the proffered signature with the specimen. This method is based on the assumption that the person makes his signature reasonably the same way each time and no one else is capable of making such a similar signature.

As the use of the signature expanded, it became the symbol of genuineness. Medicines and foods often had the maker's signature printed on the label. Currency would carry the signature of the treasurer of the issuing government. The signature seemed to lend credibility, even though it was printed. With the popularity of the signature came forgers. As mentioned above, it was assumed no one could make the signature of another person. This is, of course, false. Given time, practice, and some training, anyone can become a fairly good forger. The trick with forgery is to produce the fraudulent signature at the same brisk pace that the true signer does and still make it look like the original. There are many people–some of them in jail–who are quite good at this. However, since signing a good forgery with the quick motion of the true signer is infinitely more difficult, it became the practice to ask that the document be signed in the presence of the paying party. Often a document already signed once would have to be signed again, so that the party in authority could witness the typically fast, smooth strokes of a person signing his own name.

Thus, the signature became the symbol of ID as well as commitment, but it was still necessary for two parties to come together if the forger was to be defeated. This led to an early electrical device, a *telautograph*.[1] This system comprised two similar devices, connected via telephone lines (Fig. 1). Each device consisted of a mechanical pen and a pad or a roll of paper. The pens each had two arms connected to their point, running to electrical control sensors beyond the edges of the paper at the other ends. As a person signed on the paper, using the mechanical pen on the transmitting machine, electrical impulses were sent along the telephone lines. The receiver, at the other end of the lines, made its pen move and left a

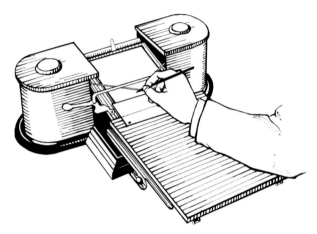

Figure 1. Original telautograph machine used to transmit signatures for identification. (Sketch by Benbrook)

mark on the paper identical to the trace at the transmitter. The speed, rhythm, and shape of the inscription at the receiver was close to that at the transmitter. The received inscription, however, did not effectively reproduce varying weights of line or pen-tip pressures. This led some users to keep a file of signatures as received via Telautograph, as well as signatures made by a normal pen. This method was effective in sending signatures over wires and could also be used to send any other kind of written information. Many Telautographs are in use today, and the product, much improved in recent years, is still marketed.

MESSAGE AUTHENTICATION

In systems where teletypewriters are used for conducting business, a signature is not a practical means of ID. For these systems, code words known only to certain parties are used to identify the sender. Often, these codes are changed daily or even with each message. Such codes have been in use ever since the teletypewriter was first used. Some of the more complex codes are used in banks and financial companies and are closely protected secrets. The code method usually provides for a change of schedule if any of the parties has reason to believe the code might have been compromised.

MASS IDENTIFICATION

In the last twenty years, with the coming of consumer credit and widespread use of checks, the businessman has found it necessary to identify his customers. This social change has made business ID a new game: mass ID.

Although mass ID does not lend itself well to either code words or signature-comparison ID, both are in use today. It was natural for the business community merely to expand the methods they had been using within their closed systems and install them for credit cards and check cashing.

Since it is impossible for each merchant to maintain a signature file on all potential customers, the customer is given a plastic card and asked to sign it with a specimen signature. The customer carries this card in his wallet as a reference signature. He then presents this card to the merchant when he signs the sales slip. This method, then, puts the signature file in the hands of the public, and the comparison is the responsibility of the merchant. The credit grantor is hardly in the picture.

The code or password is also in use for customer or mass ID. It is called the *personal identification number* (or PIN number). A four- or five-digit number is given to the customer when he is issued his plastic ID card. (Some systems permit the customer to choose his own number.) This number is recorded at a central file, and the customer is asked to memorize it. Thereafter, each time the card is used, the customer is asked to enter his PIN number into a keyboard. This entry is transmitted to center and compared. If a match results, the customer is considered to have been identified. While the PIN is satisfactory for the customer with one card, it would be awkward for a person to memorize a number for each card in his wallet. The business and financial communities are still seeking a good answer to mass ID. In the meanwhile, the signature and the PIN will have to suffice.

POLICE IDENTIFICATION

Police ID has had a different history. While business transactions are as old as man, organized police systems are quite new. London founded its first police force, on the action of Sir Robert Peel, in 1829. New York City followed with a similar organization in 1844. The first state police organization was the Texas Rangers, established in 1835. Not until 1908 did the Department of Justice form what later was to become the FBI.[2]

With this late beginning, police ID progressed rapidly and has developed into a skilled profession using sophisticated technology. It has surpassed the business or transaction ID many times over.

The first serious effort at a technique of identification was the Bertillon method of classifying physical characteristics (Fig. 2).

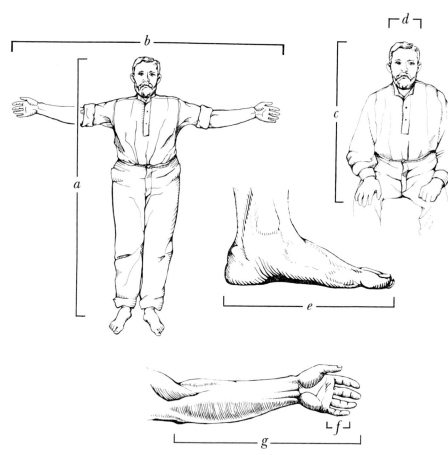

Figure 2. The Bertillon method of criminal identification was by physical measurements: *(a)* height, *(b)* span, *(c)* trunk height, *(d)* head width, *(e)* foot length, *(f)* finger length, and *(g)* forearm length. This was used from 1870 until World War I. (Sketches by Benbrook)

This system, formalized in 1886, listed the length of the arm, lengths of fingers, height, and trunk–eleven distinct physical measurements in all. It was designed to seek out those characteristics one could not change; thus, it could be applied successfully to the uncooperative identifyee. This made it ideally suited to police work.[3]

Bertillon's system, called *anthropometry,* was a big step forward, but was destined to reign for only twenty years. A now-celebrated case of two prisoners, both named Will West and having identical Bertillon measurements, occurred in 1903. These two men looked so much alike and measured so nearly the same that they were assumed to be one person until they both appeared at the same place; in prison. The proponents of the then new fingerprint system had the men printed, and there was no similarity whatever.

FINGERPRINTS

Following a number of anthropometric errors, the fingerprint system was suggested as a replacement.[4] The criticism of Bertillon was that there were, indeed, duplicates. Enough was known of fingerprints to realize that there were never exact duplicates and that fingerprints did not change with age. Accordingly, the fingerprint system soon replaced the Bertillon method in almost all police ID during the period prior to World War I.

Except for improved inks and some more sophisticated classification methods, fingerprint ID did not change much until about 1965. At this time, there were some attempts to introduce fingerprint methods into the transaction ID area. There were a number of marketed optical and electronic devices that compared a single print with a reference print on a card. The method was similar to the signature-comparison system, in that the person carried a plastic card with a reference print embedded in the plastic. The comparison was made optically and in some cases by electronics. None of these methods were satisfactory. One fingerprint method merely put a single print on the document (charge slip or check) and retained it for record. No attempt was made at comparison unless the document turned out to be fraudulent. This met with considerable success as a deterrent, and it is still in use.

In police work, the computer became an important part of the fingerprint method. The first step was to put the classification number on computer file, so that a search could be made in minutes, rather than days. Later, by using electronic pattern-recognition techniques, the computer classified prints from ink impressions. Recently, techniques have been developed whereby the computer can scan a single finger when the finger is pressed on a glass button. The scan and comparison with a limited file takes about two seconds. There is no ink or fluid involved, and no graphic record is retained in a file.

ACCESS CONTROL

Another area where ID has become important is in access control. The concept of requiring an employee to identify himself before entering the employer's premises came into widespread use during World War II. It was a requirement for all plants engaged in defense work that employees carry ID cards. These were to be checked by guards at the entry gates to prevent sabotage. Most plants continued the practice after the war, to protect their own property from vandals and cranks. Now, the new privacy laws again make it federal law to have employees in critical areas show an ID. The critical areas are nearly everywhere that a computer can be accessed if the computer has personnel records on file.

The computer has been applied to all aspects of ID, replacing the human effort wherever possible. It has been used to analyze face photographs, profiles, signature patterns, voice, and to compare for matching symbols in a file. Although people do not generally like the thought of a computer analyzing something as personal as their appearance or their signature, it is inevitable that it will come. The computer is much faster and more accurate, and it is not subject to bias or influence, as a human judge would be. Yet, in a court of law, the computer's judgment is usually considered secondary to human opinion, especially if the person is speaking as an expert.

The field of identification will change rapidly in the next decade. After all, identification is merely the acquisition and analysis of data, and new technologies to acquire and analyze data are constantly being developed.

REFERENCES

1. Schreiber, B.: Writing with electronics. *Telecommunications.* Dedham, Massachusetts, *12(4):*73, 1978.
2. Kelley, C. M.: Message from the director. *FBI Law Enforcement Bulletin, 46(7):*1977.
3. Harris, G.: *Treatise on Law of Identification.* Albany, New York, Bender, 1892.
4. Galton, F.: Personal identification and description. *Nature (Lond.):* *38(6):*171, 1888.

Chapter 3

SOCIOLOGICAL IMPACT OF IDENTIFICATION

MANY PEOPLE CONSIDER that, since they are one of a large group, it is their right to remain anonymous.[1] It is a position that is difficult to understand. These people resent being asked to identify themselves when approached either in a public area or, most certainly, on private premises. Thus, the frequent demand for identification in today's society causes these people constant irritation.

It is even more difficult to understand the attitude these people have toward being identified by a machine. They seem to think that identification should be a negotiated process; that they should be allowed the chance to deceive the effort. (Yet, these same people consider themselves scrupulously honest.) Realizing that it is impossible to reason or argue with a machine, unattended ID stations cause these people deep resentment. They even object to devices that aid a person in making a correct ID. Again, the attitude seems to be one of sensing an unequal chance in what they think should be an unbiased adversary situation.

This attitude, which may affect as many as three adults in ten, stems from four sources:

1. Perceived rights under the Constitution of the United States.
2. The American heritage as a frontier country, where escape was always easy.
3. The nature of some aggressive people, who challenge any authority or any request.
4. Past experience with meaningless and excessive demands for ID.

THE RIGHT TO REMAIN ANONYMOUS

The so-called right to anonymity does not appear in the Bill of Rights, the first ten amendments to the Constitution. It is, however, implied in many ways, since identifying oneself to an authority might cause one to choose not to exercise one of the rights stated.

Since it was the intent of the Bill of Rights to assure the continuation of democracy, these rights must be exercised constantly or the democracy will fail. If any sociological event, such as constant requirement of ID, suppresses the exercise of those rights, it repeals the rights, and they have then lost their value. Viewed in this context, the claim that anonymity is a right does not seem so unreasonable.

Henry Goldberg, in speaking before the United States computer industry said, "[George Orwell's] *1984* is really a state of mind. If you are always tied to the consequences of your past activity, you will probably adopt a 'don't stick your neck out' attitude. This could create pressure toward conformity, which would, in turn, lead to a society in which creativity would be an early victim and the democratic ideal of a citizenry with control over its own destiny would not flourish for long."[2]

Goldberg reflects the fear that excessive surveillance could water down democratic rights to the point where principles would drown. In addition, surveillance is meaningless without identification; they are inseparable.

If some people think they have an implied right to remain anonymous, how does that affect our thinking? We must consider what ID is, in the mind of the one who believes he has this right. To him or her, ID is usually going through an act in response to a request. The act is producing a card or a driver's license or perhaps signing a register. It may be envisioned as giving a fingerprint, and this usually involves reflections on an incident in jail or in the military; both often involve unpleasant recollections. At best, the identification process, as it is known today, is not something a person wants to do, and at worst, it may be emotionally distasteful. This means that, as often as once a day, this person is upset by someone requesting ID; violating, in his opinion, his rights.

If the occasions on which ID is requested continue to increase, this group of persons will become increasingly upset. It is also likely that many new recruits will join the group. Eventually, the forces of revolt will be built up. If a democracy still exists at that time, these people could easily pass a law that did, indeed, give them a right to remain anonymous. Such a law, without other extensive sociological and legal changes, could make law enforcement nearly impossible. Thus, it would be beneficial if our society found some way to avoid alienating these people by repeated requests to identify themselves. We need some way to govern our actions and to assign responsibility and yet allow these people their so-called "right" to remain anonymous.

THE OPPORTUNITY TO ESCAPE

It was not unusual, just a few generations ago, for a family to have a "black sheep." Usually, this person was away in some unknown location. Not only was the place unknown to the family, but the person was unknown to those in the new environment. Whether or not an alias was used was immaterial, because one was seldom called upon to present identification. Without being identified, a person could disown his past and start life anew. Because of the customs of the times, these fugitive black sheep were usually young or middle-aged men running from some minor crime or from a difficult business or family situation. Because these people were not called upon to identify themselves, it is impossible to estimate how many "runaway" people there were, but they were not unusual in those times.

In some instances, a man might have escaped from unfortunate situations three or four times in one life span. There is no way of knowing how many of the black sheep succeeded as good citizens in their "next life" or how many criminals repeated their acts many times over. Society tolerated it: The community from which the black sheep ran was glad to be rid of him, and the new group was always ready to accept another pair of hands to help with the labor. Until he was proven to be undesirable in his new environment, he was welcome. If he reformed, he might stay on indefinitely.

Another form of escape was as a member of an emigrating group. The United States was founded by groups who wanted to leave a bad situation and come to the new land. No one asked for passports when the ships full of colonists arrived at the shores of the New World. No one asked for ID when a parcel of land was assigned to an owner. These people found many unpleasant situations in their new surroundings, but the harassment of identification was not one of them. Even after the government was established, there was always the frontier. People continuously moved west, where no one challenged the past and no one asked for identification.

THE CHALLENGE OF AUTHORITY

Some people oppose any request. These people bristle when asked for ID, even though they may see the reason for it. As with the group that thinks identification violates their rights, these people suffer an emotional stress when asked for ID. If asked repeatedly, they are in a continual state of upset and tension. While this state is of their own creation, society would do well to find some way to avoid antagonizing these unfortunate people.

PAST IDENTIFICATION EXPERIENCE

The biggest cause of resentment toward ID is a bad previous experience. Anyone who leads an active life has more than once come up against a bully who demands to know, "Who are you?" Quite often, he does not need to know and may not even be in sufficient authority to back up his request. Experiences like this tend to condition us to a feeling of distaste whenever we are asked for identification. We carry over the attitudes caused in us by the bully and apply them to anyone asking for an ID, no matter what their manner.

More often, the bad experience is the result of overkill. In many plant locations, employees are asked for detailed identification that is out of proportion to the security requirement of the area. The employees resent the time and bother of the ID procedure but are powerless to alter the requirements.

The experience may occur when a purchase is made on credit. All the merchant really needs to know is whether the bill will be paid. He does not need to know who the customer is. However, because of the way credit business is conducted, the easiest way for a merchant to be sure of payment is for him to identify the person receiving the merchandise. Sales clerks untrained in ID methods frequently insult the buyer in their efforts to be sure. This is an embarrassment that is not easily forgotten, and the customer will react unpleasantly the next time, even though he may be in a different store.

REACTION TO FINGERPRINTS

There seems to be a distinct, negative reaction on the part of the general public in regard to fingerprints. This could relate, as previously mentioned, to a bad experience in the military or at the time of an arrest. The fingerprint is a favorite of police officers and the armed forces and is often used excessively. Past experience cannot be the sole reason for the negative reaction, however. Even those who have never previously been fingerprinted feel that they are suspected of some wrongdoing, merely because they are asked to submit to being printed. Perhaps the movies and novels (as well as post office bulletin boards) give them this feeling.

In the fall of 1973, a test was conducted to determine the attitudes of credit card users toward fingerprints as identification. The test was conducted for Master Charge® in the San Francisco area. The conclusion, although not strongly negative, was that it was not satisfactory as a method of ID for credit card transactions.[3]

Another test conducted in Columbus, Indiana; Orlando, Florida; and Rego Park, New York was simply a one-question survey. The question-statement concluded, "Would you object to having your thumbprint taken?" The preface described that it was in connection with a credit card purchase, and an inkless method would be used. The customer, however, did not have the experience of having his print taken. Of the 300 questioned, almost 100 percent said "no objection."[4]

THE PIN NUMBER

A new wrinkle in our adult life is the PIN number. A combination to a safe can be written on a plain card in one's wallet. If the wallet is lost, it is unlikely that the finder can locate the safe and open it. Even though the finder knows the code, he can not find the safe. With the PIN number and a plastic card (in the wallet), however, the finder can empty the credit account at any retail store.

The PIN as a method of ID seems to have aroused no animosity —just disgust. The method is most popular for use at unattended twenty-four hour banking facilities. No one objects to the principle, but they find it awkward to remember. The newer systems permit the customer to select his own number. He usually chooses a number already familiar and thus avoids the memory problem. What if a person had to remember one number as an employee, another to gain entrance to his apartment house, and another one for each credit card? It would be an impossible task. Most people would either give up or write the numbers down somewhere, thus defeating the purpose. A write-up about ID for automatic paying machines for banks stated, "Surveys have indicated that about 70 percent of the people carry this [PIN] number around in written form, physically close to their plastic card."[5]

To attempt to use one number for more than one type of identification would solve the memory problem for the cardholder, but would create new ones for the system. For example, a credit card with a one hundred dollar limit at one store is a much lower risk than a universal airline's credit card. The store would not have the same protection over their file that the airlines would. Yet, the common number would have only the protection of the lowest echelon. The store would not want to go to the expense of protecting its file just for the sake of the airlines. There would also be the problem of notifying all parties when a PIN number had been compromised. This could be extremely difficult if the number were used by a federal employee for plant entrance ID and also was his driver's license ID in his state of residence.

No matter how sweetly it might be sugared, the adverse impact of the PIN number on the daily lives of the public will not be tolerated beyond a few more years.

IDENTIFICATION AND THE COMPUTER

It may surprise some readers to learn that almost all of the recent ID technological progress has been in computers. The PIN number is a derivative of the password, but it is all numeric, in entering the data into a computer via a ten- or twelve-key keyboard. Fingerprints, voice, photos, signatures–all of these long-standing ID methods are now undergoing computerized testing.

This means that identification will become fast and cheap within the next few years. With improved programs, computer ID is expected to be far more accurate; that is, with fewer errors than ID based on human judgment. Thus, with the coming of fast, cheap, and error-free ID, it is assumed ID will be required more often.

Those who remember the errors of the first computerized billing invoices and bank statements will be concerned over computerized ID. It was embarrassing to be billed for someone else's merchandise, but to be identified as someone else is unacceptable. Finally, the business world has reached the point where computerized billing is more accurate than it was initially and can even be called more accurate than the manual billing processes of twenty years ago. Certainly, computerized ID systems will reach the level where they are more accurate than a human, but during the early years there will be seemingly unforgivable errors. These will not be taken lightly, and there will be lawsuits and, no doubt, criminal cases before the courts.

IDENTIFICATION AND PRIVACY IN CORPORATE DATA BANKS

The ability of a computer to store great quantities of information is well known. It is easy to load in increasingly more data, and it is equally easy to access it. Even though safeguards are usually taken to protect sensitive data, a computer is unable to judge who should get what data. It does not know when to yield to a request and when to refuse. The computer is a machine of obedience, not a machine of judgment. Today's computers are usually accessible from dozens of terminals at great distances from the computer room itself. To keep close security on the computer room is meaningless if the computer data can be accessed from the next state.

There are two principal ways for an unauthorized person to gain access to a computer data base. One is for him to gain access directly, by deceiving the computer into thinking he is authorized, and the other is to tap the telephone lines while a properly authorized party is in contact with the computer. Good system design has password control to prevent the first case. By using cryptographic techniques for transmitted data, the second method can also be blocked. The password is, of course, a method of identification.

Cryptography is not involved with ID, except that it may be used to prevent someone from intercepting the passwords.[6] Most systems have a set of passwords, each one assigned to its own data base. These should identify the requestor at least as one of an authorized group, and preferably as a particular individual. The time of the request, the terminal used, and, of course, the operator should all be logged on the computer activity log. It is not enough that the person be identified as one entitled to access; his name (not his password) should also be logged.[7] The passwords should not be related to the data sources in a hierarchical fashion, i.e. a given level should not be entitled to his own data and all other less classified data. The passwords should only be for one type of data. If certain persons are authorized access to many types of data, they should be assigned many passwords. Alternatively, the passwords may be assigned one to each person–thus being truly an ID tool. Then, those types of data that that person is authorized to use could each have that password on file. Some files might have many names and some names might appear on many files, but each person has a unique ID password, and only one. The degree of sophistication required depends on the risk involved–not solely on the value of the data. The risk must be evaluated before the security and ID policy can be formulated.[8] The important elements of any security system are identification and logging.

The above discussion pertains principally to corporation computer nets where payroll, personnel records, corporate sales volume, and other sensitive data is on file. Usually, few people are assigned passwords. If necessary, these people may access files for other employees, who need only occasional contact with the data base.

IDENTIFICATION AND PUBLIC DATA BANKS

For large files of sensitive data, such as bank balances or hospital medical records, the problem of privacy and ID is quite different. In these cases, only the involved party has a right to the data, yet that person does not have a terminal and probably does not know how to operate one. In most of these systems, a clerk reads the data from the terminal and passes it on to the customer or patient. In such a case, the clerk has a password and identifies the involved person by an ID card, usually one issued for the purpose. Thus, the difficult problem of privacy and ID is overcome by identifying two people.

One system now in service involves tens of thousands of persons and over fifteen thousand terminals (Fig. 3). In this system, operated by First National City Bank of New York, the customer directly interfaces with the computer.[9] He may inquire as to his

Figure 3. This modern terminal is used by the public to inquire about bank accounts. First National City Bank of New York has thousands in operation. Identification is by PIN number. (Photograph courtesy of Transaction Technology, Inc., Los Angeles, California.)

bank balance without going through a clerk. The terminals are simple to operate and relatively inexpensive. Of course, the customer is limited in the number of transactions he can perform.

In this system, the customer is identified first by the possession of a card and then by a three- to six-digit PIN number. The card itself is unique to the banking industry, in that it does not use the magnetic stripe for memory. To operate the terminal, the customer first puts his card into a slot. This advises the computer system of the account number. Next, the customer enters his personal identification number in the ten-key keyboard on the terminal. Then, to get his account balance, he enters a single digit into the keyboard. His dollar balance in his account can be read on a small numeric display much like the readout of a pocket calculator. The system handles millions of transactions per month. The bank is planning an increasing number of instances where the general public will be permitted to work with the computer system. To assure privacy, the computer must identify the party before sending out the data, via the PIN number.

Some systems make use of the Touch-Tone® telephone as a terminal. These are popular in "pay-by-phone" systems for bank customers to pay utility bills. The need for ID in bill paying is not as great as in balance inquiry systems. Still, to prevent errors, each customer is given a PIN number. This must be entered via the Touch-Tone keyboard before any transaction can be accomplished. The ID in the systems using a telephone for a terminal is not as good as in the systems using a card-activated terminal. Once an imposter has obtained a PIN number, he can enter the system from any of the 140 million telephones in the United States. In systems using proprietary terminals, there is added protection, because the imposter must first steal a card and then go to a terminal. This is a distinct security advantage in the identification process.

IDENTIFICATION FOR OBTAINING GOVERNMENT MONEY

The unhampered growth of government social programs has made fraud against the government a major drain on the taxpayer. In the decade of 1965 to 1975, the food stamp program grew from 400,000 recipients ($36 million) to 19 million recipients ($5.2 billion). The combined food stamp, social security, disability insurance, retirement and survivors insurance, medicare payments and Aid to Families with Dependent Children totaled $31.9 billion in 1976. Most of this is issued in monthly or bimonthly checks; thus, the recipients understand the system quickly. Often, no ID is required at the time of application for benefits, permitting one party to apply repeatedly. The use of false identification at the time of application occurs most frequently in the food stamp and Aid to Families with Dependent Children programs. There is almost no use of false ID in the social security programs at the time of application.

There seems to be no sincere effort at control of these programs. The State of Massachusetts was found to be issuing food stamps without any apparent monitoring. Not one case was found in which the state made claims against the believed ineligible recipients in the three-year period of 1973 to 1975. Yet, a federal audit turned up that 50 percent of those receiving stamps were ineligible and many used false identification. Utah, however, pursued 378 cases in this same period and recovered $103,000 in false payments. Not surprisingly, their ineligibility rate was found to be only 3.1 percent when an audit was made.[10]

The major fraud problem in the social security program is not in applications, but in the cashing of stolen checks. There is a feeling among those cashing checks that a government check is risk free, because it is drawn on the United States Treasury. Indeed, the check is good, but the presenting party should be required to identify himself as the proper holder. In Philadelphia, prior to the crackdown on lost and stolen checks, 10,000 welfare checks per month were issued to replace those reported missing. Of the missing checks, 4,000 were subsequently cashed.[11]

It is unlikely that the federal handout will diminish, but there must be some means of controlling the fraud. The losses are not exactly known, but they are in the tens of millions of taxpayer dollars. It seems likely that proper ID would be the first step in reducing the fraud.

ALIEN IDENTIFICATION

The Immigration and Naturalization Service (INS) of the federal government is responsible for supervision and enforcement of the federal laws concerning aliens. They have outstanding about 5 million Alien Registration Receipt cards. The INS also estimates that there are 8 million illegal aliens currently living in the United States. Most of this group have false ID of some form, to avoid being caught and deported. As long as the United States is such a highly desirable place to live, compared with other countries, the illegal alien will continue to be a problem.

To maintain records on aliens, the INS issues visas (immigrant and nonimmigrant), and border-crossing (green) cards. The immigrant visa is intended to permit an alien to come to this country with the intent of becoming a citizen. The quotas are clearly limited by law, and the requests are usually granted only to those people who have close ties with United States citizens or have a skill that would make them valuable citizens. The nonimmigrant visa is a temporary pass issued to travelers, students, employees of foreign government facilities in the United States, or businessmen. It is in this group that the problems of ID occur. They too often use their legal short stay to obtain false identification papers, and when their "legal" term is up, change their names and remain in this country.

The green card is a temporary work permit issued to Mexican citizens. Thousands of these are issued every year, and thousands more are counterfeited. The INS now has a new alien identification card involving fingerprint, photo, signature, and code that should reduce this counterfeit traffic sharply. These are now under test and will be issued over the next few years.

DRIVER'S LICENSES

To most teenage persons, a driver's license is the most important document in the world; a sign of adulthood. This is an understandable attitude, since it is issued only after proof of a certain age. The fact that our society considers it the most genuine ID also lends strength to this attitude.

The reason for the value of the driver's license as an ID is that it (all of the fifty states and the District of Columbia licenses) carries some physical description of the driver and is thus not readily transferable. Over half of the states have antialteration techniques built into the license. Some of these are only plastic coatings or the use of safety paper; others are sophisticated coded films over the face of the card. Generally, counterfeit licenses are so easy to obtain that alteration is not worth the effort. Many young people carry two driver's licenses; one is official and regarded as an operator's license, and the other has the birthdate marked back a few years. The second one makes them appear more adult and is usually dated so it allows them to buy alcoholic beverages. A criminal will have one or two others with false addresses and names. These "alias" cards are used for credit purchases and check cashing.

IDENTIFICATION AND TODAY'S SOCIETY

It is apparent that today's society requires that everybody carries with him a means of identification at all times. Most people

TABLE I

SECURITY RELATED TO ID SYSTEMS*

Security Level	Requirement for Security Breach	Example Basis for Identification
Minimum	No forgery needed	Code-only system
		Household quality key system
	Straightforward amount of forgery	Card system
		Sophisticated key system
		Card-code system
	Readily duplicatable personal attributes	Personal appearance system
		Hand geometry system
	Difficult-to-duplicate personal attributes	Voiceprint system
		Fingerprint system
Maximum	Presently nonduplicatable personal attributes	Genetic code system

*From C.W. Swonger, *Application of Fingerprint Technology to Criminal Identification and Security Systems.* Read before the First International Conference on Electronic Crime Countermeasures, Edinburgh, Scotland, July, 1973.
Courtesy of C.W. Swonger.

carry multiple means. Each situation seems to call for a different level of security, and a different type of ID. Table I shows the hierarchy of ID methods in use. With a transient population of 36 million people changing residence in a single year, with national retail credit available to over 50 million households, with check volume at 100 million items per day, it is a different world than it was immediately after World War II. To those people whose values are those of the first half of the century, the need for ID seems foreign and even unpleasant. As that generation phases out, carrying and proffering identification documents will become less of an irritation.

Figure 4 shows a mapping of inquiry rates versus data base size, with probable areas of future environments for identification systems.

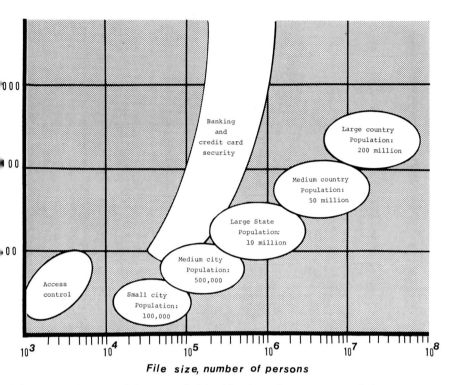

Figure 4. The potential automatic-identification clients, as extended to an entire populace, is mapped. Estimated inquiry rates run into thousands per hour. (From C. W. Swonger, *Application of Fingerprint Technology to Criminal Identification and Security Systems.* Read before the First International Conference on Electronic Crime Countermeasures, Edinburgh, Scotland, July, 1973. Courtesy of C. W. Swonger.)

Perhaps new technological means of ID that are less cumbersome than current IDs will be developed. The public will demand that the techniques be suited to the need, and that one will not have to give a life history to cash a check. At the same time, positive ID in protecting sensitive computer records from unauthorized eyes is obvious. The public will accept lengthy ID in this area. Certainly, there must be improved ID for obtaining government funds. The prevalent welfare fraud must be controlled, and ID will play an important part.

If "the good guys" are to be differentiated from "the bad guys," it will be necessary to have better ID. To stop the job drain caused by illegal aliens, the selling of liquor to underage persons, and the smuggling and selling of illegal goods, both the criminal and the honest citizen must be identified.

Identification cannot be done with the laws and methods of the past. Laws concerning privacy are recently on the books and will be interpreted in the courts very soon. New techniques for ID are now available and are described in this book, and more are being developed. With these new methods, a new attitude is needed, so that we can handle our rights and responsibilities intelligently in modern society.

REFERENCES

1. Berkowitz, L.: *Aggression: A Social-Psychological Analysis.* New York, McGraw, 1962.
2. Goldberg, H.: *Impact of the Less-Cash Less-Check Society.* Read before the Computer and Business Equipment Manufacturers Association Seminar, Washington, D. C., May, 1975.
3. Warfel, G. H.: Test is made of fingerprints for Mastercharge verification. *Payment Systems Newsletter, 7(1):6,* 1975.
4. Ahern, R. A.: Inkless thumbprinting. *CARD 1(3):* 1977.
5. *An Assessment of Less Cash/Less Check Technology.* Cambridge, Massachusetts, A. D. Little, 1974.
6. Katzan, H.: *Computer Data Security.* New York, Van Nostrand Reinhold, 1973.
7. Courtney, R. H.: *A rational approach to data security.* Read before Electro '77, 1977.
8. Courtney, R. H.: *Security Risk Assessment in EDP Systems.* Poughkeepsie, New York, IBM, 1975.
9. Glaser, P. F.: *Card Services.* Read before the Payments System Symposium, New Orleans, Apr., 1978.
10. Feltner, R. A.: Statement before Committee on Agriculture and Forestry. Washington, D. C., (U. S. Senate, Nov., 1975).
11. Federal Advisory Committee on False Identification: *The Criminal Use of False Identification.* Washington, D. C., U. S. Dept. of Justice, 1976.
12. Swonger, C. W.: *Application of Fingerprint Technology to Criminal Identification and Security Systems.* Read before the First International Conferences on Electronic Crime Countermeasures, Edinburgh, Scotland, July, 1973.

Chapter 4

FUNDAMENTALS OF IDENTIFICATION

SINCE THE TASK of identification has not been a commercial effort, there has been little analytical thought given to it. Modern society seems to bring the analytical guns to bear only in those places where it is believed that shortcuts will reduce cost. Typically, when a job becomes isolated and is assigned to a specialist, the next step toward improvement is in trying to reduce cost.

Identification in business use has not had isolation, but, rather, has always been assigned as a related function, perhaps to the guarding of an entrance, cashing a check, or selling merchandise. Not until these functions were automated and identification was isolated, as a singular function, was it analyzed as a task. Also, in social situations, one seldom stops to realize that identification is a conscious act. Not until we are confronted with the inability to do it do we concentrate on identifying someone apart from all other thoughts. At this time, it should be realized that the process is so nearly automatic that we cannot intentionally call up a technique for identifying a person. We realize we cannot break the task into subtasks and how little we actually know about the process and how inadequate it is.

Consider someone you see only twice a year, perhaps your doctor, some member of a club in which your spouse is active, or a family relative. You will recognize that person in an instant, but can you describe that person so a third party would recognize him? In the law enforcement area, this is a common problem; the victim is unable to describe his assailant, but can readily pick him out of a lineup. It is surprising that such an important skill as recognition has not received more attention from the philosophers and psychologists. No one seems to be able to tell how identification is performed.

IDENTIFICATION IN FOUR CIRCUMSTANCES

Why is identification important?

35

There are four general reasons why it might be necessary to identify another person. These are listed below, with a discussion of each of the four. They include, briefly, social, transactional, access control, and forensic situations. There is a great deal of overlap, as the discussion shows, but these "short names" suffice.

Social Situations

1. Why is identification important in a social situation? *So one may become involved with the other person with a knowledge of his background.*

In a social situation, this may be only so that one may converse with him. Voices are pitched differently to people of different backgrounds. Selection of words, sentence construction, inflections, and, of course, the choice of subject matter is aimed at the listener's background. If the person has not been identified, conversation is difficult.

Picture yourself in a room, with the knowledge that there is someone sitting beside you, but hidden by a curtain and forbidden to speak. It may be a stranger, a friend, or perhaps one of your own family. It may be an infant, a youth, or a dying invalid. It may be someone of the opposite sex. Not knowing, how would you address the person? Once the person is identified, you can provide him with pleasing, if one-sided, chitchat. Until then, you "don't know where to begin."

With this situation in mind, it is obvious that identification means more than a name. If the other person is a stranger, knowing the name is "Pat Smith" is of little help. Yet, if Pat is known from a previous meeting, a conversation may begin. Thus, in a social situation, identification means some knowledge of a person's background, and this knowledge permits one to successfully become involved with that person.

Usually, others can be identified on sight. Even if their name cannot be recalled, their background and interests come to mind. In this case, appearance is helpful. The other person's appearance may put him in a readily identifiable class. One would not converse on the same subject or in the same fashion with an elderly clergyman that one would with a college girl. Just on sight, a limited degree of identification has permitted at least an opening to a conversation. Where outward appearance does not give a clue, conversation is begun on a common subject, such as weather or some item from the current news, and then explored. After a few minutes, the interests and background of one's friend is established, and one has some factors of identification.

It is most frequently the case that identification is performed, perhaps subconsciously, so that one may become involved with the other person. In this case, the term *identification* means more than the person's name; it means some facts about their life-style and past experience. If a "social" introduction is only by name, this single fact must call up more detail from memory, or the identification is inadequate. Frequently, the introducer appends a factor to the introduction that permits a conversation to start. The discovery process can then begin, and soon there are enough facts for a social identification.

Transactional Situations

2. Why is identification necessary to a business transaction? *So one can plan to commit to some future relationship with the other person.*

In this case, the identification need not refer to any past experiences. The intent is to establish, in the other party, a commitment to perform at some future time. Actually, the identification is only so the person can be located in the event of default. In this case, the ID consists of enough data that it provides us with the answer to "Where can I find you if you default?" In situation 1, the ID was for "How can I successfully converse with you?"

Business identification usually involves providing one's name, address, place of employment, age, sex, and marital status. Frequently, this means filling out a form, such as an application for credit or membership in a club. Following World War II, when the world population was drifting about almost aimlessly, these applications were used for more than simple identification.

The forms asked questions that put the applicant into a class or category, and often the request was granted on a class basis. During this period, applicants for credit or banking relationships were asked if they had been divorced, about their race, how many residences they had occupied in the last three years, about their

education–numerous questions that had no bearing on the need
to enforce the commitment involved. These questions were used
for credit scoring, a method of rating an individual's financial
worthiness based on national averages. Each factor in the application was weighted, then a formula was applied, and the application
was granted according to a numeric factor. The questions involved in this aspect were treated separately from the straight ID
questions, but on the face of the application form, they appeared
to be all the same.

With the aid of a good program and good computers, credit
scoring became a useful tool.[1] Because of the close interrelation-
ship with identification, such numeric processes became a target
of the privacy champions, and, by the enactment of laws, were
soon reduced to a low level of effectiveness. Further, the Equal
Credit Opportunity Act and Federal Reserve Regulation B restrict
the use of the two prime factors of credit scoring and identification:
age and sex.[2] If these are eliminated from application forms, credit
scoring becomes difficult and identification impossible. If the form
clearly states that it is used only for identification, these facts may
be included. Thus, application blanks evolved from simple ID forms
to complex personal histories and then regressed back to simple IDs
in a span of thirty years.

The upsurge of bank consumer credit has produced much fraud
in applying for credit. The skilled con man finds it easier to obtain a credit card by fraudulent application and then use the card
frequently than to falsely identify himself for each use of the card.
What the trade calls "false apps" is now the second largest source
of fraud loss in the credit card business. The privacy laws may
soon push it into first place.

Although the credit-granting and credit-checking organizations
have formed a close fraternity as a matter of survival, they are less
than honest with each other about the methods used to detect
fraudulent applications. It is generally agreed that a driver's license
is poor evidence, and a birth certificate is worse. There seems to
be no accepted "best" ID, but much trust is put on the ID of other
credit grantors. Such trust is not misplaced, especially if the previous application is a year or two old and bears a picture and the
address has not changed. It is well to check that the address exists

and that it is a residence, not a mail drop. The applicant can be asked to describe the building (duplex, apartment, brick, frame single residence, etc.) as a means of verification. If a phone number is given, it is wise to call the number. Is the applicant known? Is it an answering service?[3] Patience and judgment are required to properly pursue the facts given in an application for a job or for a credit account. Usually, the effort pays off. One false application can use up the profits of dozens of valid ones.

Access Control

3. Why is identification important in issuing privilege cards (access control)? *The person is to be permitted a privilege not generally accorded to all.*

Again, as in situation 2, the identification is mixed with some other feature, usually a qualifying act. In the previous case, the qualifying act was a financial status (not really an act, but certainly a condition). Here, the qualifying act may be past performance, such as passing a test or accepting restrictions and responsibilities, perhaps as a condition of employment.

The driver's license is an example of an ID that bestows a privilege and requires the passage of a test. Since the privilege is not to be transferred, the license carries extensive identifying information. Because of the wide distribution of the driver's license and its detailed ID data, it has become the prime ID document in the United States, even though it is known to be unreliable. As it is used increasingly for ID, more identifying information is being added. Today's driver's license has become principally an ID document, and secondly, a vehicle operator's permit.

An employee badge, while it may not require a test, requires that the identifyee qualify as an employee. In some plants, the badges (or cards) have a hierarchy of privileges. For example, all badges permit access to the parking lot and the main lobby. Some, furthermore, permit access to the administrative area, while others do not. Still fewer allow the holder to go to the executive floor, and very few fit the slot outside the computer complex. Each cardholder must qualify for his own level of access.

Club membership cards identify the holder as entitled to enter and use the facilities of the club. Originally, the party had to qualify to be a member in most clubs, but today's laws concerning discrimination have removed almost all barriers in private clubs. The elimination of sex, race, and age limitations have left the exclusive clubs with high fees as their only means of establishing commonality among their members.

In the above cases, the document issued to indicate the right to certain privileges carried identification data to prevent its transference. In each case, the card or badge was issued to an individual, and its use was restricted to that individual. Even though many others had the same rights, many did not have these rights, and to keep the members of the former group from passing the card to the latter group, identifying data was put on the document. These, then, were documents identifying the individual as a member of the group.

There are also situations in which a person may be identified as one who has a certain right that no one else has, yet anyone could have been given that right. For example, a hotel room and its key: The key carries no indication as to who is assigned the room, but the use of the room is limited to the one to whom the key is issued. A similar situation exists in car rental. The use of the car is not to be transferred from the original renter, but minutes after the car is returned, it is rented to another person. In such cases, it is not customary to ask for personal identification before issuing the keys, beyond that necessary to assure payment. (The car rental requires a valid operator's permit, which also carries identifying information. In addition, a rented car can be taken away and never returned. For this reason, identification of the renter is of interest. It is not possible to steal away with a hotel room.)

Some municipalities are issuing taxpayer ID cards or residence cards and requiring them for access to public parks. These may or may not contain ID information. If they are to be signed, it is usually only to prevent them from being used by a nonresident should they become lost and then found. The park supervisors certainly do not care who you are, only that you are one of the group qualified to enter the park. Similarly, the ID cards proffered by maintenance craftsmen who call at the home to make repairs do not need to identify the repairman as a person. He need only assure the householder that the repairman is deemed honest by his employer and that he is capable of making the repair.

Until recently, the evaluation of the identifying information was always by a person in contact with the identifyee. Now developing is a situation that requires identification in a location where the identifyee is remote from the identifier. This occurs in computer nets where the data base and the computer main frame are located centrally, with many terminals located remotely. The computer can be operated from these remote terminals, and the data can be accessed from them, too. Thus, the computer itself must perform the ID, since only the identifyee is present at the remote keyboard. There are many tricks used in doing this, all of them based on passwords of some nature.

In this case, access to the computer and certain data are granted to the person only after he types in his password. Certainly this is not identification. Anyone having knowledge of the password can operate the terminal. Of course, this method provides some security, but does not tell in any way who is operating the terminal. By changing codes frequently, the method can be kept reasonably secure, and it is always policy to issue new code words when it is suspected that one has been compromised. The computer access control is an area that needs immediate attention, so that privacy of records can be maintained.

Forensic Work

4. Why is identification important in forensic work? *It is necessary to prove that the identifyee is the party that performed a prior act.*

This may be as simple as determining that the person has paid his bill, or it may be proving a suspect guilty of murder. These are vastly different degrees of gravity, and, of course, they are surrounded with different degrees of proof of identification. In each case, however, it is necessary to associate a prior act with an individual.

The simplest form of forensic ID is a receipt. For a receipt to be an ID document, it must carry the names of the payor and payee. Then, if there is doubt that the document is in the proper hands, a secondary form of ID may be required. Identification of this type occurs thousands of times per day and never gets to court. A person may have a commuter ticket issued to his name, and if the conductor has cause to question the validity of the ticket, he may ask the rider to show identification of some nature. If the identification item has a photo that matches the rider and bears the same name as the ticket, the conductor is satisfied. The use of a commuter ticket not your own is prohibited by law, and thus might become a forensic situation.

A more detailed document, and one that is self-sufficient, is the plastic student-body card. It indicates that the person has enrolled and paid tuition. It usually carries enough identity data, perhaps a photo, to obviate the need for any supporting ID.

There are many documents, tickets, passes, chits, script, etc., that represent prior payment, but are transferable. These items do not carry any identifying data, but may have extensive anticounterfeit data. These may be presented by any person, not necessarily the original purchaser. The tickets may be limited and assigned, as in reserved seats for a performance or for air transportation, or they may be mass-issued, as in urban transit tickets or tokens. There are also passes that do not carry ID information and cannot be transferred outside of the group, issued to a limited class of holders. Riding pool parking passes often indicate the driver of a pool, who can be any one of four or five members. The pass merely identifies the person as the one driver for that day and allows him to park any vehicle he is operating in the designated place. Thus, the driver is identified as one who is permitted to park a car, but it might be any one of half a dozen cars or any of the group of drivers. The driver is one of a closely limited and adequately identified group.

The most celebrated cases involving identification with reference to some prior act are, of course, in the courts of law. When one speaks of identification, most people think of fingerprints, law, and crime. Although identification in law enforcement starts with the earliest investigation, it often ends with the jury having to decide on the adequacy of the link between the criminal act and the accused. To this end, many hours are spent in detective work, in preparation of evidential data, and in briefing witnesses; all proving that the accused was the one who committed the crime.

The methods and technology involved in identifying suspects are highly developed. Most large police departments have crime laboratories equipped to take latent fingerprints, analyze handwriting, make castings of footprints and tire prints in soft earth, and examine toolmarks and firearms marks–literally hundreds of tests. These involve the skills of highly trained specialists in chemistry, electronics, and optics, all with a background in criminology. For the smaller police organizations that cannot afford a complete lab, each state operates an available facility. The federal government provides access to many crime labs, subdivided by region and by governmental department. In addition, many universities have laboratories for teaching, with professors willing to act as expert witnesses in criminal cases. There are consultants and private examiners operating as independent experts in the complex area of identification. These men often have a background of experience that is greater than the government employee, because they focus their interest in specific fields.

In forensic investigations into the identity of a person who is suspected of committing a previous act, there is a great deal at stake. The task of positive identification is further encumbered by the unwillingness of the suspect to cooperate and by the laws protecting a defendant. In an effort to see that trials are fair, laws have been structured to make it difficult for the police to gather data without infringing on the defendant's rights, thus having hours of valuable work eliminated from the acceptable evidence. The gathering of identification data for a court trial is a delicate and time-consuming task. To build a good case requires the best equipment and trained experts.

IDENTIFICATION RELATED TO RISK

In all cases, the degree of effort spent in identification should be related to the risk. The "risk" in making an error in identification is a complex factor. If erroneous ID is made, the cost of performing ID is wasted. Furthermore, whatever action was taken on the erroneous advice may also be a total loss, as in cashing a forged check. It may not be a loss if there is recourse and recovery; then, the loss is the cost of recovery. In addition, there is the effect of the error on future challenges. If it is known that a certain method of identification is never wrong, it will not be intentionally challenged. Thus, there is a strong deterrent factor, which reduces the risk to near zero. If a certain method, however, is known to have frequent errors, it will be challenged more often, with more frequent success. The deterrent is an important element in computing risk.

As mentioned before, in a court of law, identity must be proven "beyond a reasonable doubt." There are also certain business transactions where the risk is high and identification must be completely accurate and must be recorded. Other transactions are of such low risk that simple recognition is sufficient. In most employee access identifications, it is enough to know that the person is one of the group employed on the present shift at the location involved. For high security areas, however, exact records are kept on who entered the premises and when. Exit logs are also kept. Even in social identification, a more sincere effort to identify someone is made if it seems important. Often, the degree of importance associated with the person is directly related to the embarrassment that might be suffered if we were wrong.

In a business transaction, it is not only easy to evaluate the risk of error, but most observers agree on the risk figures. In social or forensic situations or even in employee access control, it is difficult to evaluate the risk of making an error in identification. In all cases, the effect of deterrent must be considered. Even a poor system would be rated high if it successfully inhibited any attempt at challenge.

Using as an example a credit card transaction, examine risk versus the cost of ID. Figure 5 shows the risk plotted vertically, and acceptable cost is plotted horizontally. As the risk increases, so does the acceptable cost. Note that the risk is not equal to dollar value. Real estate and groceries are at the same low level of risk. This seems an unlikely pair. Real estate is low risk because of deed and title registration. It is almost impossible to sell real estate that does not belong to you. Groceries are low risk because people hesitate to eat food that is not obtained from legitimate vendors. They fear it might be spoiled or otherwise unfit. In American society, food is seldom stolen and almost never fenced. Thus, food and real estate dealers are in the same class of low risk. Slightly

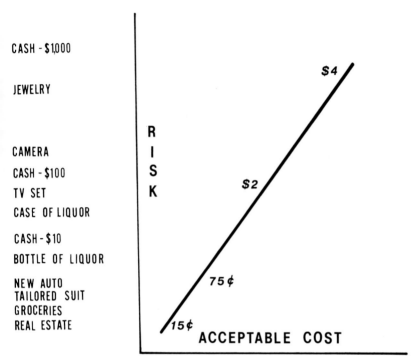

CASH - $1,000

JEWELRY

CAMERA
CASH - $100
TV SET
CASE OF LIQUOR

CASH - $10
BOTTLE OF LIQUOR

NEW AUTO
TAILORED SUIT
GROCERIES
REAL ESTATE

Figure 5. Acceptable cost of identification as a function of risk. Note that risk and value are not directly related. (From the author's sworn testimony to the National Commission on Electronic Funds Transfer, San Francisco, December 17, 1976.)

higher in risk is a new auto. Again, state registration makes it difficult to sell a car that has not been legitimately obtained. However, since it is mobile, the risk of transference of ownership between inadequately identified parties is somewhat greater than in real estate. Buyers also seem willing to enter into slightly shady automobile deals. A tailored suit is also difficult to sell to anyone other than the man it was measured for, because of fit; hence, it is a rather low-risk transaction.

A credit card transaction involving bottled liquor is a risky transaction. A person using false identification can buy a bottle or two with a stolen credit card and readily sell the liquor for nearly its retail price. There is a ready market in "hot" liquor. Paying out $10 cash to a person with questionable ID is still a higher risk to the merchant. Most retailers would pay 75¢ to be assured of the identity of persons presenting $10 to $25 checks for cash. Note, however, that they would not pay one hundred times that for a check valued at one hundred times greater. The reason lies in two factors: (1) the relative infrequence of $1,000 checks for cash and (2) because the bad-check passers know they will be asked for verifiable ID when cashing a $1,000 check. Thus, there is a deterrent effect due to high value that actually reduces the risk.

The chart shows an estimated acceptable cost of 15¢ for identifying a party buying groceries or real estate with a credit card. And, at the level of risk equal to cashing a $100 check, a typical merchant would pay $2 to be sure of the identity of the signer of the check.

Thus, *the cost of identification should be related to the risk.* This axiom is relatively easy to see in business transactions, as in the above examples. It is harder to see in social situations or in access control, because risk is difficult to evaluate. Once the risk is evaluated (and the cost of ID is easy to establish), the axiom is seen to be true.

DEGREE OF IDENTIFICATION

A second axiom concerning identification relates more to the tolerance of the identifyee. Obviously, any act of identification involves at least one person, i.e. the one being identified. Usually a second person, the identifier, is also involved. If an identification method is to succeed, or even survive, *the degree of identification should be consistent with the need.*

First, the meaning of degree must be understood. *Degree* means a combination of difficulty and what the identifyee perceives to be the accuracy. These two constitute the physical and emotional "hassle" the identifyee suffers. If he is asked to go through a long routine and then wait while a response is obtained, he may become impatient. The other extreme is a situation in which the identifyee was not even aware that he was being subject to an identity check.

It is unfortunate that there is so much overkill in identification situations today. This excessive degree apparent in many places occurs because ID used to be performed only by law enforcement agencies. In booking a suspect, the identifier and identifyee immediately assume adversary roles, but with the officer in a distinctly superior position. Thus, if the procedure seems inconvenient to the identifyee, he is not in a position to object, nor, in most cases, does the officer care. Today, these same procedures and often the same people (ex-police officers as security agents) perform ID procedures in situations that do not require such methods, and the result is excessive identification.

A test in which a fingerprint was taken at the time of a credit card purchase was once conducted.[4] The method was not costly and was a slight inconvenience to the customer. He was asked to press his finger on a corner of the back surface of the sales ticket he had previously signed. It was an inkless process and only took five seconds. Since it was a test, the thirty merchants involved were asked to request the thumbprint on every Master Charge sale during the test period, but the customer was allowed to refuse. Under no circumstances was the merchant to try to coerce the customer, and the sale was to be consummated whether or not a print was obtained.

The public acceptance was surprisingly high, with only a few customers preferring not to be printed. However, as part of the test, four hundred people were interviewed concerning their attitude toward the method. Nearly one out of four people indicated that if one credit card system required fingerprinting and another did not, that difference would cause them to use the latter card. Fingerprinting for a credit purchase of a few dollars seemed to be too high a degree of ID for the situation.

In considering the degree of ID, the identifier must also be taken into account. Although the identifier is an employee, if the method is too long and complex, the result can be a disgruntled staff and lowered employee morale.

THE IDENTIFICATION PROCESS

The task of identification is always a two-step process. One step involves data from the identifyee when he is known and the other when he is not yet known. The steps usually occur in the order stated. In a forensic situation, if the suspect has no previous record, even fingerprints are useless until the suspect is apprehended. In this case, the evidence may have many good latent prints taken at the scene of the crime, but no one knows whose prints they are. Then, when a suspect is booked, reference prints are taken from the known suspect. If they match the latents, identification is made.

In most transactions and access control situations, the reference data is logged at the time of enrollment. This occurs when the account is opened or when the employee is hired. This file is then used for comparison each time the identifyee is called upon to identify himself. Thus, the identifyee states who he claims to be, and the system verifies that he is right or declares him to be an imposter, by comparing the instant data with the data previously logged.

ERROR RATES

Any system is subject to error. In most systems, there are many graduations from correct to incorrect. But in an identification system, there are not graduations; the system is either right or it is wrong. This is because the systems are verification systems and not true identification methods. This means that someone (usually the identifyee) makes a statement identifying the person; then the ID system says the statement is true or false. The ID system, then, verifies the statement as to who the person is.

In court, even when the identifyee may be dead, someone states who the person is supposed to be, and then the statement is technologically proven right or wrong. Although this means the system has no graduation, it also provides the opportunity of two kinds of error, called by various names.

The purists, using statistical terminology, refer to the case where the method erroneously says the initial statement is false as a Type I error. When it says, in error, the statement is true, this is a Type II error. This is cumbersome to all but those experienced in statistical notation, and improved terminologies have been generated. One, uses IPR (impostor pass rate) to indicate a Type II, and FAR (false alarm rate) as a Type I. Again, this is confusing, because it assumes that a rejection is an alarm. A much easier terminology was introduced by the author in 1975 by merely calling the two errors *false accept* and *false reject,* as opposed to *true accept* and *true reject.* If the system makes a mistake, it obviously either falsely confirms the statement or falsely denies the statement (as to who the identifyee is claimed to be). In doing so, the system either falsely accepts or falsely rejects the identifyee. Of course, if the system operates properly, it either accepts or rejects the statement and the person properly. It is unfortunate that false-accept and false-alarm rates have the same initial letters and yet mean opposites. Usually, however, the false alarm notation has included the word *rate,* and thus is abbreviated as FAR. This book uses FA and FR to indicate the types of error. If these are expressed as a percent of total, the word *rate* is assumed.

In any system, it is desirable to reduce the errors to as low a level as possible. In a system such as a verification system, where there are two type of errors, one must further strike a compromise between the two error possibilities. Figure 6 shows the unavoidable dilemma of an increasing FA, occurring with an attempt at reducing FR. This is a basic perversity of verification systems.

Some experimenters have taken the percent error at the point where the FA and FR curves intersect in an effort to evaluate

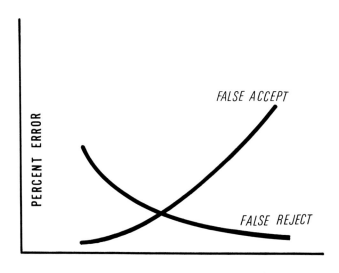

Figure 6. A decrease in the false accept rate of an ID system will cause an increase in the false reject rate. A high-security access control functions best near the left side. For customer check cashing, the right side is more acceptable.

ID systems. This yields one figure, and it is a good relative guide as to the capability of a system. By making FA equal FR, all systems under consideration are judged at the same point. However, few systems are expected to operate at this point. It is similar to evaluating household heaters at an ambient temperature of zero degrees. While it provides a standard, it is too demanding a method for use in the sunshine states of the South and inadequate as a reference for northern climates. Another common rating is a total of FA plus FR in percent. This method assumes identical test conditions for all systems under comparison. An ID system involving the public can afford a method that allows a relatively high ratio of FA to FR. This is because the system itself deters most people from challenging it, and a high FR would soon turn public opinion against the system. For a high-security system or for cashing high-dollar checks (or selling expensive, easily fenced merchandise, such as jewelry), the ID system should have a low FA rate, even at the expense of a high FR rate. In this situation, the users expect a high FR and tolerate it because they know they are putting the identifier in a position of high risk.

The author has proposed a rating based on the ratio of FA to FR. In the above examples, the check cashing of a high-dollar amount would call for a FA-to-FR ratio of 1 : 200, or 1 : 400, depending on the the risk. Yet, identifying the general public might require a FA-to-FR ratio of 1 : 20. The FA-to-FR ratio in a real estate transaction reflects the low-risk situation in a positive integer, such as 10 : 1 or 20 : 1. These values are shown in Figure 7, where the vertical scale is identical to Figure 5, but the horizontal scale is the FA-to-FR ratio instead of cost.

To establish the FA-to-FR ratio of a system, it must be put through many tests. Half of the tests must be a challenge to the system, i.e. persons acting as imposters. The other half must be persons claiming their correct identity. Each half must be in sufficient volume to allow a leveling off of the error rates.

As an added factor in evaluating identification (or, more accurately, verification) systems, this ratio could be related to the number of identifications in the sample base. In this case, the ratio would not be reduced mathematically, but it would indicate the number of FAs and FRs that could be tolerated, or occurred, in

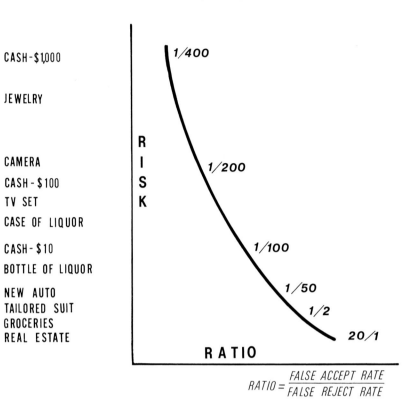

Figure 7. Ratio of accept-reject errors as related to risk. (From the author's sworn testimony to the National Commission on Electronic Funds Transfer, San Francisco, December 17, 1973.)

the sample size stated. For example, in a high-risk situation (the $1,000 diamond watch sold via a check) the number of FAs should be 1 in 10,000; the FRs, 500 in 10,000. The figure for the system of identification should be 1/500/10,000, and for a lesser risk, such as a case of liquor sold via a credit card, 1/100/5,000. Accepting a personal check for groceries is of such low risk that the ID system could be rated 10/1/10,000. As before, the test base should be one-half false-accept attempts (forgeries) and one-half false-reject attempts.

In the first case, an FA cannot be tolerated. An FA rate of 1 in 10,000 indicates that it is nearly impossible to breach the ID system. The FR rate of 500 in 10,000 (1 in 20) indicates that the identifyees understand that the system is geared to near zero FA and thus has an unavoidably high FR rate. The merchant must be patient in explaining this and have alternate means of establishing the identity of those initially rejected. The FA to FR in this case is 1 : 500. The sample size of 10,000 represents more than a lifetime in the average jewelry store.

The second case still has an understanding clientele, because most people realize the risk in selling liquor on credit. Thus, the FA-to-FR ratio is 1 : 100. Since the dollar value is under one hundred dollars, an FA ratio of 1 : 5,000 is quoted. The sample size represents about two years in a neighborhood liquor store.

The last case shows an FA-to-FR ratio of 10 : 1 in a sample size of 10,000. If 10,000 represents six months of checks cashed at a grocery store cash register, the grocer can tolerate ten bad checks because of false ID, as long as he only insults one customer by falsely suspecting him of forgery.

The above examples and the numbers involved demonstrate the rating system. In actual practice, the ratios depend on the competitive situation, the nature of the customer base, and the type of neighborhood.

COMPATIBILITY

The attitude of the shopping public and the customs of business generally determine the actual figures. This leads to a third axiom: *The ratio of false accept to false reject must be compatible with the risk and the customs of the business involved.*

This axiom, although it uses the word *business,* applies to all cases of identification. Even in a social situation, one must not inquire to the point of being rude, merely to identify someone. At the other extreme, in legal matters, some instances require fingerprints and others only a notarized signature for proven identification. In every "business" where ID is involved, there are customs and standard procedures that must be respected.

THE BASIC METHODS OF IDENTIFICATION

It has been said in many reports that identification can be established by one of three basic methods:[5, 6, 7]

1. What a person *has*–an artifact such as a key or a card.
2. What a person *knows*–a password or memorized number or recall of some past incident.

3. What a person *is*–a physiological trait, such as a fingerprint.

The following should be added:

4. What a person *does*–a grip, a stride, a signature, or a hand sign or word spoken in a particular fashion.
5. What a person *recognizes*–an image selected from a group or a photo chosen from many random photographs.

It is the author's opinion that to identify a person by what he has, a mere possession, is not truly identification. It is not even verification or authentication. The fact that a person has a key does not identify him as the owner of the house, even if the key fits. The possession of a card does not mean that the person was necessarily issued that card; he may have stolen it. Unless the card is related to the cardholder in some fashion, such as a signature, a photograph, or a memorized password, the card does not provide ID.

The use of what a person knows is better as ID, but is still not proof. If what is known could be taken from the rightful knower, either by threat or by observation, then an imposter could succeed. If the knowledge were taken by threat, of course, the original knower would be aware that the secret was out and take steps to block its use. If the knowledge were taken surreptitiously, the secret would be presumed kept, and the imposter could repeatedly succeed.

An artifact such as a key or a card can be stolen, but it is missing from its original place. When a password is stolen, it still exists in the mind of the first person; thus, the theft has resulted in a counterfeit duplicate. The knowledge can be readily passed on; duplicates are free, and their existence cannot be detected until they are used. It is difficult to accuse a man of possessing stolen knowledge, and proof is impossible. The possession of a stolen or counterfeit card or key, however, is excellent evidence of guilt, even though the thief may never have had the opportunity to use it.

"What a person is" presents a good case for ID. It is for this reason that fingerprints are widely accepted as positive ID. While fingerprints can be forged, it is a difficult process that often fails. Other physiological features can be used for ID. The Bertillon system of identification (see Chap. 2) used eleven body dimensions as identifying characteristics. Finger length can be used, and facial features can be compared to a photograph. Any feature that is relatively permanent and not changeable at will can be used to provide ID.

To some, "something a person is" includes signature and voice characteristics.[7, 9] These, however, can be changed and are mostly the result of a learned pattern, not a given trait. It is true that certain resonances in the voice are unchangeable and that signatures depend to some extent on finger structure that cannot be changed. It is the author's opinion that these two personal characteristics belong in the category of "what a person does." This category includes those acts a person does so automatically that they take on the quality of unchangeability, yet they may be, at least in part, subject to controlled change.[8] Most personal characteristics under the heading of what a person does, are a mixture of what the person knows and what the person has.

The last component, *recognition,* is a derivative of "what one knows," but may be incapable of transfer. The password or memorized number is easily transferred from the proper holder to an imposter or an agent. If the known item is an indescribable blob or a mess of scratches, however, these may be recognized and mentally identified from a field of similar but not identical images and thus provide secret ID. The concept of an identifyee establishing his identity by something he recognizes has not been widely developed, but it is a method that is more secure and easier to retain than passwords or PIN numbers.

It has been suggested by SRI International that extra security be gained by using two or three of the basic components in combination.[5] The addition of a photograph (something a person is) to the plastic card (something a person has) increases its security, as does the addition of a signature (does) or a PIN number (knows). SRI claims the security or resistance to fraud of such a multimodal system is the product of the two component securities. If a PIN number is breached once in five hundred times and a card fraudulently used once in two hundred times, the protection of the two should provide a breach rate of 1 in 100,000 times. Although statistically true, using a straight multiplication of the factors in a multimodal system does not take into account the focused efforts of an impostor. Certainly, a criminal in possession of a PIN number is going to make a pointed effort to get the card that matches the number, rather than steal thousands of cards on the random chance that one will match. Even before the multimodal method was presented in a paper on security, it was in use in all cash vending machines and automatic tellers in the United States. All of these machines required a card and a PIN number, although a few have come out now without cards.

CHOICE OF BASIC COMPONENTS

For simple entry control, or even for low-risk retail transactions, to determine that the identifyee has a card, a pass, or a key is enough. Compromise can be minimized by annual reissue and a clear statement of the expiration date on the face of the document. Further protection can be gained by having the holders report when the artifact is lost or stolen. If all issued items were identical, as in the case of a key, it is then necessary to reissue to all holders. If the items were unique, i.e. all carried a name or number, then a notice to all acceptors listing those cards reported missing should soon pick up those in the hands of unauthorized persons. Such a list is used by most credit card issuers and acceptors, as is the annual reissue policy.

To tie a card or paper document to the proper holder, often the item bears some trait the holder is or does. A face photo or a description, for example, make it difficult for an imposter to use the item. To use such a method, the acceptor must take time to check the user against the item. Even if the acceptor does not actually check each person, the potential is there and an imposter will hesitate to chance being caught using stolen ID. A photo or description on a pass or a badge provides infinitely greater security than one carrying a simple number or even a name. Because of the lack of attention on the part of most acceptors or identifiers, most of the increased security comes from the deterrent aspect. It is of little concern to the acceptor where the security rests, and it is always welcome.

The use of a physical description as something a person is, is no longer popular. Because most people tend to stretch the truth, the terse, factual blanks about height, weight, and hair color, have caused resentment. Most men tend to think they are taller than they are and most women think they weigh less than they do. Although all seniors acknowledge grey hair every time they look in a mirror, they do not like to see it printed on their driver's licenses. The antidiscrimination activists have vigorously campaigned against recording race or sex on an ID document. No one over thirty seems to want their age printed out. Thus, the description is yielding to a photo as a means of recording physical characteristics. Perhaps the average person is more capable of matching faces to photos than at guessing height and weight. With or without reason, the description figures are vanishing from ID documents.

MACHINE IDENTIFICATION

With the trend toward unattended ID, the basic components that can be machine read are increasing in popularity. Certainly something one has is easily machine read. The brass key is machine read by the key slot in which it is used. The plastic card with holes or magnetics on it is usually machine read. But, what a person knows is impossible to read by machine, or even a human, without the cooperation of the identifyee. The human identifier, of course, asks the identifyee to speak what he knows, as when the bank clerk asks for a mother's maiden name. In so doing, the identifyee gives out the secret to anyone within earshot. For unattended ID, the PIN number is frequently used. The identifyee indexes the number into a ten-key pad for a computer to read and compare with the file. A code word can be similarly used if the key pad had alpha characters on it, as with keyboard telephones. To machine read something a person is presents a problem in sensing the trait. People are wary of having a machine contact them for a height measurement or to sense facial points in a profile. Although weight can be taken without unaccustomed contact, the intrapersonal variation in weight is not widely different from the interpersonal variation; thus, it is not a good characteristic for a large population.

The two personal characteristics (something a person is) that are being read by machine today are fingerprints and finger length. The print reading requires expensive equipment; the finger-length quipment is quite reasonable. Neither have seen widespread use, ut may come into their own with improved technology.

The component "something a person does" has tremendous potential in the area of machine ID. By doing something, the identifyee takes his characteristics to the machine. He can impart something of what he knows, is, and has. Breakthroughs can be expected n this area in the next few years. If the known part is easy to remember, or already known, and the physiological part is sufficiently intrapersonally constant, the possessed artifact can be the familiar plastic card. Such a system should be acceptable to the public. Economics and time to perform are two aspects that technology must solve if "something a person does" is to succeed. The trend is hopeful.

FEDERAL IDENTIFICATION

A rather frightening result of the failure of private industry to come up with a good ID method is the interest the federal government has shown. As mentioned before, the Immigration and Naturalization Service is now testing a card for aliens that carries a multitude of ID features, all tied together in a machine-readable code. If Congress ever decides that it is necessary to provide all citizens with identification, it will be easy to duplicate the card for each person. The disturbing part is that, for most situations, this card is overkill. It lends itself to varying levels of ID, but how can we be sure a complete identification procedure would not be required just to buy a monthly bus ticket? The fear is that pompous bureaucrats would soon be recording life histories at every turn. This thought causes us to hope that a good identification means will soon come forth from the private sector of society. It was heartening to see that the Federal Advisory Committee on False Identification focused on the need for a general ID technology but recommended against a federal ID system.

To leave the chore of identification in the hands of private business means that every individual may be involved with many different types of ID. While this has its disadvantages, so does a common ID. If all credit cards elected to use the same PIN number but issued different levels of credit, chaos would result from the varying degrees of security at the various card data centers.

It would be preferable to have a different ID method for each use than to have them all the same. Yet, to memorize a PIN number for each card would require an above-average memory. Perhaps a better system is in the offing.

CONCLUSION

There are some complex problems yet to be solved in the field of identification. The solutions involve the basic component methods: what a person *has, knows, is, does,* and *recognizes.* The need for machine reading makes it essential that a person carries a card or badge, thus involving the basic component of what one *has.* A good system involves another component, and the most likely one is what one *does,* because it can utilize both what one *knows* and *is.* (What one *recognizes* is not yet a developed component.)

The need for identification is a current problem, as a result of a mobile, yet closely integrated, society. The fundamental technology is available. A system that is acceptable to the public in convenience and economical to use must be designed.

REFERENCES

1. Roy, H. J.: Breakthrough in credit scoring. *Stores.* New York, NRMA, 1973.
2. Ambrose, J.: Flaws in credit scoring highlighted by 'Neil' Butler of FRB. *Nilson Report.* Issue no. 164, May, 1977.
3. Investigative outline. *Fraud Application Control Seminar.* San Francisco, TRW Credit Data, 1977.
4. Ryan, M. and Schorer, P.: *Customer Reaction to Thumbprint Authentication of Bankcard Transactions.* Western States Bankcard Association, San Francisco, California, Apr., 1974.
5. Raphael, D. E. and Young, J. R.: *Automated Personal Identification.* SRI International Report. Menlo Park, California, SRI, Dec., 1974.
6. Ferdman, M., Lambert, D., and Snow, D.: *Security Aspect of Bankcard Systems.* Read before the American Bankers Association, Louisville, Kentucky, Sept., 1975.
7. U. S. Dept. of Commerce, NBS: *Evaluation Techniques for Automated Personal Identification.* FIPSPUB-48. Washington, D. C., NBS, Apr., 1977.
8. Warfel, G. H.: *ID: Where Are We Now?* Palm Springs, California, I.D. Code Industries, Inc., May, 1977.
9. Woods, H. M.: *The Use of Passwords for Controlled Access to Computer Resources.* Washington, D. C., U. S. Dept. of Commerce, May, 1977.

Chapter 5

FINGERPRINTS AS A METHOD
OF IDENTIFICATION

T HE USE OF THE PATTERNS of the friction skin to identify a person dates back many centuries. No doubt the earliest man noted that the parts of the body used for grasping (feet and hands) had minute skin ridges, whereas on the rest of the body the skin was smooth. It is not known when man realized that these ridges formed patterns that were different from finger to finger and from person to person and never varied throughout a lifetime.

There was general interest in the fingerprint method of identification during the early and middle 1800s, but not until 1880 were fingerprints proposed as a means of identifying criminals. By this time, the Bertillon system was well entrenched in most progressive police organizations. As pointed out in Chapter 2, the fingerprint soon won over the Bertillon system, and it is the only positive ID method currently used by police.

There are three excellent reasons for using fingerprints in forensic work: (1) There is a wide interpersonal variation in prints. To date, no two people have been found to have identical prints. (2) There is a high degree of intrapersonal consistency–even through the growth years. A person's fingerprints may change in scale, but not in relative appearance. (3) Latent fingerprints are unknowingly left each time the finger contacts a surface. While these latent prints cannot always be developed, when they can be obtained, they present sound evidence. This unintentional leaving of a trail makes fingerprints unique among all systems of ID.

As with any identification system, the fingerprint relies upon the comparison of known and unknown data. In forensics this means that the latent prints found at the scene of a crime must be matched to a suspect's reference prints. This may be done after the suspect is apprehended and fingerprinted, or it may be found that the latent prints match those of a previously fingerprinted person who is still at large. In the latter case, painstaking searches must be made while the crime goes unsolved.

Precedent in courts of law has been established to accept finger-prints of twelve matching characteristics and no mismatching characteristics as sufficient for positive identification. Like much of law, this is completely arbitrary, although it is well established through precedent. Often, these twelve points occur in a very small area, as little as 1 sq. cm. of a latent print, representing only one-sixth of a complete print. If that is all that is available and no mismatches occur within the printed area, it is convincing evidence.

Recently, the search for matching prints has been aided by the computer. There are now search systems that may introduce finger-prints as a means of transaction or entry control. To date, however, only experimental entry control systems exist, and these are in high-security locations backed up by other means. Cost and poor public acceptance may prevent fingerprints from being widely used, except in forensic situations.

CLASSIC METHODS OF FINGERPRINTING

The taking of reference prints, with the subject known and at least reasonably cooperative, is quite different from developing latent prints. The latent prints are not usually visible to the unaided eye; thus, it is necessary to treat the surfaces where prints are most likely to be found and to hope for a good print to appear. Of course, it is necessary that the surface be undisturbed since the contact was made with the finger of the wanted person, and it is important that the developing method itself not upset the latent print or the surface in the process of development. In criminalistics, this means that fingerprint specialists must be first on the scene, before any potential prints have been disturbed by other investi-gators. Of course, criminals often wear gloves or carefully wipe any touched surfaces, leaving no prints. While it is desirable to work with the prints soon after they are left, there is actually little aging of latent prints in a normal environment, i.e. in air compatible with human habitation. Obtaining a good print is far more de-pendent on the physical and emotional condition of the person, the pressure of the contact, and on the surface contacted than on the age of the print. The skill of the investigator is also paramount, because he must suit the method to the print, using all the infor-mation he can obtain before starting to develop the print.[1]

A person whose normal tendency is to perspire leaves an excellent print, while one whose skin is always dry presents a serious problem to the investigator. In addition, if the person is under emotional or physical stress, the secretion of perspiration by the sebaceous glands is greatly increased. The person with normally dry skin leaves an easily developed print, and the heavy perspirer may actually wash out his own print under the stress of committing an illegal act. One who handles large volumes of paper, such as a file clerk, develops dry hands after a few minutes of filing. This, coupled with an experienced light touch, makes the file clerk's prints difficult to develop and easily separated from the prints of the criminal who was under stress as he handled the same item.

The fingerprint expert, who has enquired and learned that the prints may be days, weeks, or years old and that the surface has been in an air-conditioned room or a damp basement or in a desert sun, has some leads to his approach. He must now be careful that his own efforts do not interfere with success. Small items, such as a gun or a bottle that may have been handled by the identifyee, can be taken to the laboratory for well-controlled print development. If the prints are believed to be on a wall or a stair railing, the fingerprint expert will have to bring his equipment to the scene. When developing prints on a paper document that may be subject to other investigations, such as handwriting analysis, the investigator must not use chemicals that will destroy the ink, thus interfering with subsequent work.

RECORDING PRINTS

Recording a set of reference prints is not a critical task, though it requires some training. Most police departments have a clerk or a junior officer trained in the skill and making record prints for a small fee. One-day training courses in taking record prints are offered by the schools that train private security personnel. These courses teach the student to make good reference prints and to recognize when the print has not succeeded and should be redone. Usually, some simple classification instruction is also given.

A typical fingerprint record card is shown in Figure 8.[2] Note that the right-hand impressions *(top row)* are in their normal left-to-right sequence, but the left hand is recorded in reverse. This

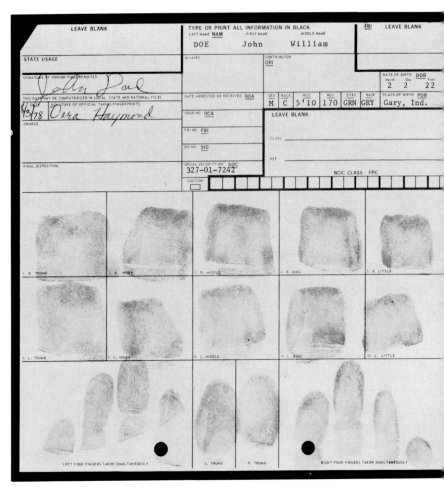

Figure 8. Typical fingerprint reference file card. Individual prints are rolled to provide prints of 80 percent of finger. Lower group of prints are taken simultaneously to show positional relationship and joint skin creases.

puts the fingers of the same name one above the other. On the lower half of the card, then, the prints are grouped in their natural relationship. The individual prints are rolled, yielding nearly twice the area and twice as much data for identification. It is essential that the lower group impression is taken simultaneously, one hand at a time, thus showing the true relationship of finger length and assuring that no error has been made in sequence. Rolling, of course, is not possible in the simultaneous prints.

To obtain clear rolled prints, it is necessary that the person making the prints grasps the finger to be printed and rolls it. The printing finger must be held firmly with two or three fingers of one hand, and one or two fingers of the other hand are then used to exert pressure, ensuring a firm impression. At best, it is awkward, and the motion is an unnatural one for the identifyee.[3] If the identifyee is disabled by arthritis or broken bones, an experienced person must take the prints using special spoon-shaped tools, with individual blocks for each print. The prints can then be assembled onto the card individually. Such special methods should always be noted on the record card to aid future investigations.

The ink can be ordinary black printer's ink or any of the special inks offered by the police equipment supply houses. Ink, rollers, slab, and forms can be obtained from National Police Supply in Charlotte, North Carolina; Criminalistics, Inc., of Miami, or any of many local shops specializing in forensic supplies.

When the ink is spread in a thin, sticky film on a smooth slab, the finger picks up ink only on the ridges, not the valleys. The same rolling motion is used in inking that is used in making the impression on the record card.

The ink should be well beyond the first crease and almost to the knuckle for the simultaneous print. Unavoidably, it is a messy process, but inadequate inking does not reduce the mess and does reduce the quality of the print. When the job is done, soap and water or presoaped tissues can be used for cleanup. The ink slab and roller should be cleaned unless they are to be reused soon. Dry, tacky ink will not give as good a print as freshly rolled ink. Because of the clean up process, most departments set aside a specified hour of the day for routine fingerprint work.

DEVELOPING LATENT PRINTS

There are two general ways to develop latent prints.[4] One is by dusting the print with a powder of a color that contrasts with the surface; the other, by using a dye that colors the print chemically. Usually, the first is used on a fresh (up to a few months in normal air) prints, and the chemical method is used on old prints or for prints on porous surfaces.

The dusting technique is the time-honored method popular in detective stories. It is also the best, in some cases. The investigator must use his judgment and draw on his experience in deciding whether or not to use the dusting method and which powder and what brush to use. Generally, powder is best on glass or metal. Powders can be obtained in many colors, the most useful being black, white, and red. These all create the print by adhering to the perspiration left behind after finger contact. To retain a permanent image, the print may be photographed or the dust may be "lifted" by clear adhesive tape. Some powders can be hardened in place by the application of radiant heat.[2] Usually, the photograph is best. Special lights can be used at slant angles, thus enhancing the image. Filters can also help bring out the image so it stands out clearly against the background. Photography is especially useful when the powdered image is on a background of varied coloring. Filters or even powders that react to ultraviolet light can be used to produce a contrasting image. It is in enhancing the image without distorting the evidence that the skill of the investigator is taxed.[1]

On porous surfaces or in cases where powders are difficult to apply (such as the underside of a built-in shelf), chemicals are an excellent aid. While powders adhere to the water in the deposited secretions, chemicals are either absorbed by or react with the solids in the deposit and color these solids. Perspiration is 98.5 percent water. The water absorbs into paper and cloth and in a few months evaporates from a nonporous surface. Powders do not yield a good print in such cases. Remaining on the surface for decades, however, are the sodium chloride and other salts, plus fat, urea, amino acids, and other organic body materials. Applying iodine vapor or silver nitrate can make the fat and oily deposits turn dark. Prints produced by these chemicals develop to maximum intensity in five to thirty minutes, depending on how directly the fluids are applied. These chemicals tend to alter any inks (pen, rubber stamp, and endorsing stamps on checks), and care should be taken not to interfere with other investigative work. Iodine is especially corrosive and tarnishes metals. Chemical prints have a short life, the iodine fading immediately and silver nitrate fading on exposure to light. Thus, it is best to photograph the prints at their maximum contrast. There are ways of fixing chemical prints and ways of lifting iodine prints, but modern photography has largely replaced these techniques.

The most used method today, rapidly replacing the above chemical and powder methods, is the commercial chemical ninhydrin.[4] This is available in a spray can, making it easy to use. The print develops almost immediately on new prints and over hours or even days on older prints. Development can be hurried by the application of steam or radiant heat. This method was introduced in the 1950s.[1] At first, the investigator had to make his own liquid by dissolving ninhydrin in ethyl alcohol, acetone, or ether, making a 1 percent to 2 percent solution. It is now available from most supply houses as an aerosol bomb. As with most liquids and sprays, care must be used. The acetone base causes inks to run, destroying handwriting evidence surrounding the print. The ether base ninhydrin does not. Alcohol base spray stains or even removes paints and adhesives, and so does acetone. If prints have been attempted with silver nitrate, the subsequent action of a ninhydrin spray will be nil, but the reverse is not true. Prints that are developing in ninhydrin must be handled with extreme care. The reaction is so quick with fresh prints that all contact must be avoided until the desired latent has been fully developed and photographed.

In addition to powders and chemicals, there are many methods used by senior members of the profession that seem to be out of date in today's technological world. Sooting directly onto the surface with a flame from resin or pine shavings and then brushing with a feather has produced excellent results when done by a skilled investigator. Shaking or blowing off excess powder is sometimes done to avoid contact with a brush. At the other extreme, there are new methods that make it a simple task to develop latents in average cases. One is the Magna® brush, available through MacDonell Associates in Corning, New York, by which a magnetic powder is applied and the excess removed by magnetic attraction. New chemicals, said to be better than ninhydrin and with a safe carrier fluid, are now being tried. These new developments could make the iodine and lampblack methods obsolete.

A chemical called *ortho-phthalaldehyde* has been tested and found far more sensitive than any previous method.[5] By spraying this substance (using distilled water as a carrier) from a medical atomizer, a print develops in minutes, where other methods have failed. The print is visible under "long" ultraviolet light (366 nm). By photographing the print with a UV filter, even a varicolored background, such as a color photograph, appears black, thus giving a high contrast to the purple glow of the ridges.

In working with latent prints, it is necessary to adhere to a sequence of testing methods to assure that one does not cancel the effect of a following test. The iodine fuming should be first. It has no adverse effect on subsequent tries. The ninhydrin should be next (or, in many labs, the iodine is omitted and the ninhydrin is first). Of the chemicals, silver nitrate should be last. Following these, powder methods can be used, selecting a powder for maximum contrast with the background.

PRESERVATION OF FINGERPRINTS

To be of value in identifying a person, the fingerprint must be recorded in a manageable fashion. It is unwise to allow anyone, even a jury, to handle evidential fingerprints in their original form.

Lifting by clear adhesive provides an original print, without destroying the perspiration secretations that created it. The 3M Corporation makes an excellent lifting tape. Today, though, photography is the usual method of preserving evidence. Little is lost in clarity by taking a photo, and, often, by using special lighting, filters, and perhaps ultraviolet powders and chemicals, the photo may show more contrast than the original image. In addition, lifting does not provide the observer with the position of the print with relation to the object contacted. The position or orientation of a print (or prints) may be critical, not to identification, but to other aspects of the case.

Any camera can be used for fingerprint work, provided it has a 1 : 1 close-up lens.[1] Most popular is the 4 × 5 that has ground-glass focusing. These versatile cameras are invaluable as regular crime lab equipment and do an adequate job on most fingerprints. The 35-mm camera is gaining in popularity because of its small size. Favrot, Inc., has a line of cameras and adapters specially designed for fingerprint work. The Polaroid® CU-5 is thoroughly satisfactory, but it is beneficial to make a permanent negative if record retention is expected. As in developing the latent, experience is vital to success in photographing fingerprints.

Fortunately, photographing a fingerprint does not disturb it in any way. Thus, dozens of shots can be taken under different lighting effects, and the best one then can be printed for evidential or record use. The print may be backlighted if it is on a transparent or translucent surface. A glossy surface can blind the camera under direct light, rendering the print all but invisible. By using a polarizing filter on the light and color-rejecting filters on the camera, a good contrast can be obtained. Slant or oblique light can be used on relief prints, such as prints in mud. To seek the optimum angle, the technician should use a ground glass in the camera and move the lights around until a satisfactory contrast is obtained.

Reproduction of record cards is a simple task for a copy camera. The records should never be copied by office copy machines, since such machines lack the necessary detail for something as critical as a reference print. Good microfilming, however, is acceptable and saves a great deal in file space. Transmission of prints by facsimile is acceptable if the facsimile is of fine definition. The average machine designed primarily for typed sheets is not adequate. The Datalog Company of Melville, New York, produces a line called Policefax®, which has one system of "message" quality (91 lines per inch) and one of "fingerprint" quality (200 lines per inch). Transmission of prints by closed-loop television is usually unsatisfactory. Television is designed for the reproduction of motion and neglects the needs of finely detailed still images. There are slow-scan TV systems for fixed images, but these are of the same resolution as the CCTV systems and are slow scan, so that the system will work on ordinary telephone lines. The design objective of such a system was economy, not detail.

CLASSIFICATION OF PRINTS

To file and retrieve record fingerprints for quick reference, the prints must first be reduced to a character group. This group of alphabetical and numerical characters then provide a search key. Providing this key to the print record card is done by classifying the prints. Some classification systems have as many as thirty (three for each finger) entries involving numbers and upper- and lower-case characters. In addition, the Henry system, which is the most used system, uses punctuation characters, such as the dash, parenthesis, and plus sign. At least two dozen systems have been devised and seriously considered by law enforcement groups, and new ones are still cropping up.[1]

Fundamental to all systems of manual classification is the recognition of certain formations in the friction ridges of the skin. There are three basic patterns: the arch, the loop, and the whorl. These are further divided into subgroups. The arch may be plain or tented, and the loop is called ulnar or radial, depending on the direction of slope. There are five types of whorl (Fig. 9): plain (target), twinned, accidental, central, and lateral pocket loop whorls.[2] Other terms frequently encountered in classification systems are islands, deltas, bifurcation, divergence, ridge count, and ridge tracing. Some systems classify on a basis of ten prints, some on five, and a few on single prints. At least one method uses the entire palm area.[1]

It can be seen from the above listing of terms that the classification of prints is a difficult task and is not easily grasped by the newcomer. Additionally, the hundreds of files in this country do not employ the same file formula, and the problem of tracing a person via fingerprints is fraught with confusion. The confusion, however, is the result of the systems men have applied. The basic patterns lend themselves to clear-cut classification and filing. The data is there, and soon a satisfactory method of computer classification will surface and be put to use.

In the United States, the principal file is maintained by the FBI in Washington, D. C. The base system, devised by Sir Edward Richard Henry in 1897, has been extended to handle the 165 million prints now on file.[4] It is regrettable that something as important as tagging and filing fingerprints is bogged down by the method applied to it. Equally unfortunate is the fact that the file is now so large that it would be impossible to revise the system. The system is not only cumbersome, but the population of prints is unequally distributed among the classification groups.

The prime difficulty in the Henry classification system is that it relies on the relative position of the fingers. Often, even with

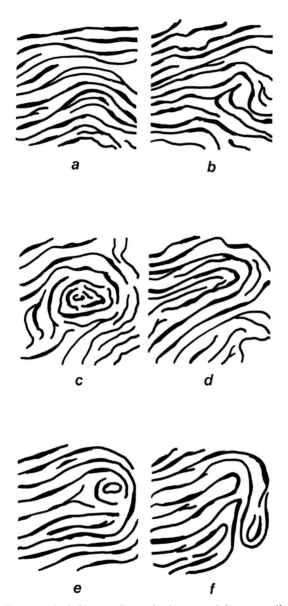

Figure 9. Some typical forms of terminology used in manually classifying fingerprints. Since the classes are by pattern and form, scale is not a critical factor: *(a)* arch, *(b)* tented arch, *(c)* plain whorl, *(d)* loop, *(e)* central pocket whorl, and *(f)* lateral pocket whorl.

three good latent prints, it is not known which hand they are from or how the fingers were originally placed in regard to each other. Yet, the Henry system uses different letters for the same pattern occurring on the right and left hands. Still another letter (lower case) is used if this pattern is on other than the index finger. In this day of computer logic, such unnecessary deviations seem out of place.

The law enforcement network of the United States has devised methods of dealing with the shortcomings of the system. When a print is found at the scene of a crime, it is first matched against all of those who could possibly have been there. This includes the victim, the innocent, the officers, and any suspects who are available to provide reference prints. If no match is found, then the print is matched against suspects not available, but who have been previously printed. To do this, the record cards are pulled and matched against the latent print. In all of these cases, the record card is pulled by name (or made afresh), and the prints are studied for a match. In many files, the cards can be referenced according to the crime involved or by the criminal's unique method of operation. These then are compared for a match with the latent prints found at the scene. Often, hundreds of comparisons are made, many of them totally remote from a match. If the system could be successfully entered from the type of print and traced to yield a name (or a small list of names), much of this effort would be saved. New York state maintains a file that can be accessed by punched cards. The classification is patterned after the Henry method. Classification is by manual effort, but the search proceeds at 400 to 500 cards per minute through IBM card equipment.

Several files are now being accessed by automated data-processing equipment. As in New York, the study and classification of the print is done by experts; then the electronic equipment handles the data, returning to the expert a list of cards to be reviewed. The prints themselves are filed in time sequence either on cards or microfilm.

AUTOMATIC PRINT CLASSIFICATION

While some of the classification errors that occur today are interpretation errors, most are the result of poor print-making.

In latents, this may be unavoidable, but in record prints, it is inexcusable. The FBI rejects over 40,000 cards each month because they were improperly recorded.[3]

One of the most difficult problems to overcome in automatic classification lies in relative size. As the identifyee grows or gains or loses weight, the fingerprints also expand or contract. While such changes do not affect manual classification, which relies on pattern form, not size, they play havoc with automatic classification. Stretching of the skin during the roll in taking a print may displace a delta from its core by as much as 10 percent. The ridge count, however, would remain the same (Fig. 10). The stretching may not be uniform throughout the print. Latents frequently show localized stretching where a small, raised area, such as the embossed characters on a credit card, distorted the skin when the card was grasped firmly.

The position of the print may cause a match to go unnoticed. Without a crease or an adjoining print from the same hand, it is difficult to sense the position of the print in regard to the hand. Algorithms can be put into the computer program, which rotates and translates the print mathematically, but these are expensive in that they consume excessive computer time.

In the area of unwanted background data (called *noise*), the computer has distinct advantages. A poorly defined latent print can be enhanced by photography (polarizers, filters, etc.), as well as electronics (Fig. 11). A threshold adjustment can be set so that "greys" below a certain level become "white" and all others

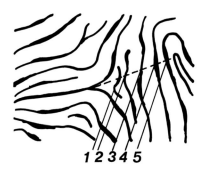

1 2 3 4 5

Figure 10. Ridge counting in fingerprint comparison. This can be done either manually or by a scanner-computer.

Figure 11. Typical electronic enhancement of a fingerprint. Although the enhanced image is less exact than the original, there is an increase in usable data and a decrease in unusable data, thus allowing a high level of machine comparison.

"black," making the print a high-contrast image. Adjustments can also be made so that a heavy print will appear with ridge lines the same width as the white valleys between them; an average of as much white as black in the print. The electronics can also be made to perform these operations on local areas where smudges or parts that seem incompletely printed tend to obliterate the detail. Reading through these areas is done by the computer's continuation logic. This same circuitry fills in pore holes or short discontinuities. While features such as pore holes are actually a part of the real finger, they do not lead to identification and are distracting to the examiner. The thin, meaningless ridges that appear between normal ridges, called *incipient* or *nascent ridges,* can be eliminated by enhancing circuitry. While such electronic tricks might seem to distort the data, far more often than not they bring out features that might otherwise have been overlooked. Many enhancements, whether they are optical, photographic, or electronic, are merely correcting for errors previously made in converting the ridge pattern to a graphic representation.

Good programming can position the print, enhance the contrast, or alter the scale to compensate for stretch or growth. Anything that can be done with optics and photographs can be done electronically. Also, these effects can be applied to localized areas, which would not be possible any other way. An enhanced image on the television screen of a computer fingerprint system is instantly available without any darkroom processing. While the operator is looking at it, the computer can be tabulating the features.

There are two lines of pursuit in the computer effort.[6] One compares the prints by optical correlations and the other by digital comparison. The correlation systems are fast in yielding a match or no-match conclusion, but do not lend themselves to rapid indexing or search. Thus, these machines will be used in a field where the identifyee wants his claimed identity to be verified, as in security access control or in transaction ID. The digital method is more suited to reducing a print to a formula, thus permitting logical search of a large file. Such systems are more suited to the forensic situations. The dominant companies in the field of automated fingerprint technology are Rockwell International in Anaheim, California, and Calspan Corporation in Buffalo, New York. Both companies participated in work supported by the FBI during the early 1970s, and both are now marketing equipment to law enforcement agencies. The Calspan system was tested for entry control by the Air Force. The false-accept rate of 2.3 percent was considered marginally adequate, but the false-reject rate of approximately 5 percent was too high.[7] Another system devised by KMS, Inc. of Irvine, California, was an optical system with mechanically controlled matching. The method was not expensive, but difficult to maintain in operating order. It is no longer being manufactured.

In manual systems, the classification is by recognition and typification of whole patterns. Once a search has reached a group of prints using this classification, the actual identification relies on abrupt discontinuities in ridge paths, called *minutiae*. With automated digital systems, the classification itself is by minutiae that have been reduced to a digital formula, and the search is conducted by matching these formulae. Andre Moenssens, in his excellent treatise on fingerprints, records eight types of minutiae.[1] He noted, however, that some experts might list only five. The automated systems use only two minutiae: ridge ending and ridge bifurcation. These, however, are augmented by giving a direction value to the ridge at the minutiae point[7] (Fig. 12). Typically, there are eighty to one hundred minutiae in a single print. By scanning the print with a fine spot of light, minutiae can be located and digitized.

The lateral position and vertical position each require 10 bits of information, and the direction requires 9 bits. Thus, an entire print can be stored on tape with 29 bits of data times the number of minutiae (approximately 100) or, under 3,200 bits. This is about 5 percent of the data in an entire print, but it is the unique and useful part. If twelve matching minutiae are sufficient for ID (with no nonmatching data), 348 bits should suffice for a court identification. This seems a ridiculous small number, when one considers that there are 10^8 bits involved in a comparison. The deception lies in the statement "with no mismatching points." To be sure of this fact, the rest of the print area must be checked.

It is believed that the digital comparison has some limitations in time and cost that confine it to a 90 percent accuracy. While this may be true for the present state of the art of computer architecture, future developments should permit a group of eight or

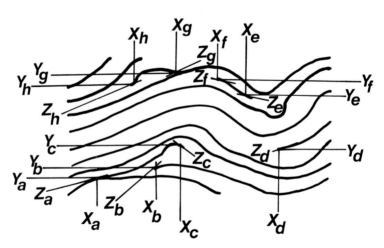

Figure 12. Digitally store fingerprint data. Note that scale and exact orientation are critical in digitally recorded fingerprints. In manually classified prints (*see* Fig. 9), form and pattern are more important.

ten parallel systems, each examining a part of a print. Such a method would be almost eight or ten times as fast, but, of course, nearly eight to ten times as costly as the present digital comparison systems. With continued cost reduction in computer construction, this "sub-area" method may be feasible.

Recently the correlation method was proposed for a new system using sub-area techniques.[9] Sub-area correlation has been successfully used in terrain matching, which is essentially identical to the problem of fingerprint matching. The proposal states that previous correlation systems have been defeated by local stretching. Since correlation systems are largely optical, it is not possible to use software to compensate for such localized errors. By breaking the print into sub-areas, the local stretching problem can be handled. Certainly a sub-area optical correlation system would be fast. Whether it is economically feasible depends on the relative cost of the new computer technologies with which it must compete over the next few years. Correlation systems require that the fingerprints be on transparencies rather than on card stock, adding another photographic step to the process.

Shortly after the FBI test terminated, a number of scientists proposed a syntactic approach to classification.[10] Theoretically, such a method would provide a more equal distribution of prints across the print groups and thus would make search less of a problem. Although a great deal of theory and experiment has been spent in this direction, it has not progressed toward a commercial product as the digital comparison systems have. It may be that the wide difference between even close matches in fingerprints lends itself to the digital method, while syntactics separates nearly identical patterns occurring in even the small files in medical research.

A recent development in computerized fingerprint analysis is in the experimental work conducted by Rectec, Inc., of Los Altos, California. This group is working, from patents issued and pending, to compare the thumbprint of an identifyee with a group of stylized patterns. The rating or correlation of the proffered print against each one of the reference group is then recorded in memory using two hexadecimal digits for each comparison. Thus the stored data is not print data, but only a group of rating figures. The work thus far shows these ratings to have a high intrapersonal consistency and a wide interpersonal separation. As in other automated systems, the data is taken from internal reflections of the thumb or finger pressed against glass.

The print is not scanned in detail, but is summed by a Fourier transform, thus minimizing the problem of orientation. In the experimental model, the system white noise is averaged out by repeated comparisons over a two-second interval. In final design, the time for ID should be under one-tenth of a second.

Perhaps research will continue in the area of machine-aided fingerprint systems for law enforcement. The minutiae are present in every print. The technology is available in many private laboratories in the United States. Only good engineering and some good systems thinking are necessary to provide the police with a system that works. In addition, there is the ever-present problem of economics.

AUTOMATED FINGERPRINT SYSTEMS
FOR EVERYDAY USE

Although the FBI fingerprint file, with its input of 500,000 prints per month, is certainly an "everyday use," this number would be dwarfed by the system for plant access or transactional ID if fingerprints were applied to these areas. If cheap, easily operated machines were in use here, each person would be printed many times per day. Rockwell, Calspan, and KMS have all tried to apply their knowledge (gained in the FBI contract) to access control (Fig. 13). The acceptance has not been overwhelming, largely because of cost.

It is surprising that the cost of an access control system should be anywhere near the cost of a law enforcement system.[11] Consider that there is no classification problem whatever and no graphic storage of prints. This is because the identifyee is willing to cooperate to a considerable extent and wants to be properly identified. This is the opposite of the attitude of the typical suspected criminal. In both access control and transactions, the identifyee is willing to state who he is, usually by a number or a coded card or a badge. The search, then, is eliminated, and the computer must only retrieve the designated file. The file, of course, is not a fingerprint but is a formula representing the meaningful and unique properties of that person's finger. The person is told which finger to use; thus, there is no need for a search of ten possibilities. Certainly, the total file is under 50,000 in plant access, and probably under 5 million in a regional transaction center. This is small, when compared to the FBI file.

Another tremendous advantage of the "everyday" system is that the file or reference data and the sample or trial data are taken by the same method. Enrollment into this system is by presenting a finger to the terminal. Requesting acceptance is by the same act at an identical terminal. This is not like comparing rolled prints

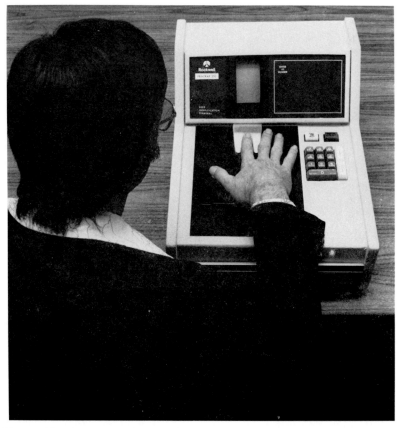

Figure 13. Automatic fingerprint terminal for instant identification. A computer analyzes the "shadowgram" of the fingertip without any ink or graphic files being used. (Photograph courtesy of Rockwell International, Anaheim, California.)

from file data, with a ninhydrin-developed latent, perhaps taken on a rounded surface.

Given all of these advantages, in addition to the acceptability of a high error rate, it seems odd that both Rockwell and Calspan priced their systems in the high tens of thousands of dollars. With improved technology and perhaps improved market research, this price should come down. When it does, fingerprints could be a factor of everyday life.

The present access control systems take the fingerprint by an optical scan of the skin as seen from the underside of a glass. The ridges, in contact with the glass, cause the area of contact to become reflective. The valleys allow the underside light to pass through and be mostly dissipated on the valley walls. Thus, a spot of light (as small as $3/100,000$ inch in diameter) scans back and forth like the beam on a TV screen. The reflected light component is photo-multiplied and presented to the preprocessor, along with the X and Y coordinates of the position of the light beam. This data is then put through enhancing circuits much like those of the forensic fingerprint computers. To reiterate, enrollment and inquiry are made on identical terminals. Thus, the treatment performed by the enhancing circuits is nearly identical in both cases. This should make the likelihood of a proper match many times greater than where the source data is a different graphical representation of the same finger, i.e. a developed latent and a record print.

Following the enhancement treatment, the minutiae are tabulated as to location (X and Y coordinates), as in the forensic systems. A comparison of these features is made with the file data. A match is an indication of acceptance. A no-match may call for a retake. Again, retake is seldom possible in criminal cases, but always available at the entry gate. A second mismatch may mean the employee (or customer) is asked to check with a security officer for clearance. With the opportunity of retake and alternative ID, fingerprints should become a cost-effective method of access control identification and perhaps become popular for transactions.

Although palm prints have always been considered an excellent means of identification, the mess of inking an entire palm has kept them in the background. Now, with inkless methods and some new reasoning, they are again of interest. It has been found that the heavy creases in a person's palm skin are unique and consistent. These creases develop in early adulthood and remain throughout one's life. Because of their size and the distance between creases, these features are easily analyzed by a mechanical or CRT scanner, thus lending themselves to computer analysis. Palm print devices should be but a fraction of the cost of fingerprint devices, once the research has laid the groundwork.[12]

INKLESS GRAPHIC FINGERPRINTS

Anyone who has been through the fingerprint process remembers well how messy it was. A number of attempts have been made at reducing this mess, all with the same degree of loss of quality. For personnel records, it might seem well to sacrifice the quality, especially when only a few prints per week are taken.

One method, called Kleen-Print®, uses a thin Mylar® film with a nearly dry ink on the back.[13] A 1½-inch square sheet of this film is suspended loosely in a cardboard frame; packaged in quantities of ten, twenty, and more per box. These are available from Precision Dynamics, Inc. in Burbank, California. After placing the film over the record card, the identifyee rolls his fingertip over the film. The film is thin enough that the ridges and valleys seem to pass through it, and an acceptable print is left on the card. The finger, however, never contacts the ink. Another method recently introduced by 3M™ of St. Paul, uses an overstamp to develop the print. The identifyee touches his fingertip to a moist pad and then touches a corner of the document, usually the back of a check or credit slip. The clerk then overstamps the area with another chemical, as he or she might do with a rubber endorsing stamp. Immediately, the two fluids react and a fingerprint appears.

The most widely used of the inkless methods is produced by Identicator Corporation in San Bruno, California. There are two models. The original product was a square box smaller than a desk telephone, in which there was a reservoir of black dusting powder. The customer was asked to press his thumb on a specified corner of the back of the check or sales slip, after the document had been properly filled out. This corner was then inserted in a slot in the box. By pressing a lever, the powder was tossed against the fresh latent fingerprint and allowed to fall away. The excess powder was cleaned off magnetically as the document was drawn over magnetized iron bars. Left on the corner was a black print. Customers were generally pleased to find that they did not have to contact any chemicals or inks, but seemed somewhat apprehensive at leaving their thumbprint behind.

Identicator now has a new method in which a dual rubber stamp resembling a doorknob is used.[14] By applying the stamp to the back of a check or sales slip, two oval spots are left, each the size of a fingerprint. One spot is solid yellow and the other solid orange (Fig. 14). The customer presses his thumb or index finger on the yellow first, then the orange. A high-contrast print develops immediately. Within seconds the spots are dry, so no smearing or overprinting can occur. As new chemicals are developed, new inkless methods appear. Recently, Signature Security Systems in Omaha, Nebraska, and Dactec International in Encino, California, have marketed inkless systems for use in personnel departments where prints are made.

All of the above inkless methods are merely controlled versions of the latent print techniques. They all produce fairly good prints;

Figure 14. Identicator method of inkless fingerprints for use in check-cashing identification. (Photograph courtesy of Identicator Corporation, San Bruno, California.)

they all have a certain amount of customer resistance. While the technologies of controlled latent techniques may improve, the customer will always be aware that he is being fingerprinted. The electronic methods that scan the finger with light seem to meet with less objection. If any of these could be made to appear that the identifyee was only pressing an "action" button and not presenting his finger for examination, the public might be fooled into ready acceptance. To achieve this, contact will have to be reduced to a fraction of a second, and position must not be critical. Perhaps such a device is being designed.

FUTURE OF FINGERPRINTS

While it has been pointed out that the general public resents being fingerprinted, for a closed group such as an employee population, it is now and will be increasingly acceptable. It is faster than a signature, does not require the soundproof isolation that voice ID does, it does not change with age and style as facial characteristics do, and it is completely nontransferable. Fingerprinting should be the principal means of access control ID in the near future. It might be an easy step from there to transaction ID.

In forensics, steady progress in the techniques of taking latent prints is expected. The arrival of a reliable machine classification and search system will probably be of the order of a breakthrough. The background now exists for a successful (though expensive) research project, as a forerunner to a first model. Because fingerprints are unique and have such an extensive legal background, they will be an important element in identification for at least the next century.

REFERENCES

1. Moenssens, A. A.: *Fingerprint Techniques.* New York, Chilton, 1971.
2. Doulder, H. C.: "Fingerprint Processing." Lecture, U. S. School of Law Enforcement, Los Angeles, Aug., 1977.
3. *Ways of Obtaining Good Fingerprints, Insuring Legibility.* Washington, D. C., U. S. Dept of Justice, FBI, n.d.
4. Vasos, S. P.: "Latent Fingerprints." Lecture, San Jose State University, San Jose, California, Mar. 1978.
5. Mayer, S. W., Meilleur, C. P., and Jones, P. F.: The use of ortho-phthalaldehyde for superior visualization of latent fingerprints. *Identification News, 27(9):*13, 1977.

6. Elección, M.: Automatic fingerprint identification. *Spectrum, 10(9):*36, 1977.
7. Fejfar, A. and Meyers, J. W.: *The Testing of Three Identity Verification Techniques for Entry Control.* Read before the Second International Conference on Crime Countermeasures, Science and Engineering, Oxford, England, July, 1977.
8. Swonger, C. W.: Access control by fingerprint identification. *Electro '76,* Paper No. 22-5, New York, New York, IEEE, 1976.
9 Ratkovic, J. A., Blackwell, E. W., and Bailey, H. H.: Concepts for a next generation automated fingerprint system. *Proceedings of the Carnahan Conference on Crime Countermeasures,* Lexington, Kentucky, University of Kentucky, May, 1978.
10. Fu, K. S. and Moayer, B.: *Syntactic Pattern Recognition of Fingerprints.* Dissertation, West Lafayette, Indiana, Purdue University, Dec., 1974.
11. Rockwell, W. F., III: Personal communication with the author, June, 1977.
12. Forsen, G. E., Nelson, M. R., and Staron, R. J.: *Personal Attribute Authentication Techniques.* Rome Air Development Center, Griffis Air Force Base, New York, Oct., 1977.
13. Barber, R.: Personal communication with the author, June, 1977.
14. Inkless fingerprints help fight bad checks. *Business Week,* No. 2472, Feb. 27, 1977.

Chapter 6

IDENTIFICATION BY VOICE
CHARACTERISTICS

O F THE FOUR CASES of personal ID (social, transactions, access control, and forensics), the use of voice characteristics in identification have seen wide application in only the social case. Certainly, it is common to hear a voice in the crowd and exclaim "that is so-and-so." It is always someone with whom we are closely associated, and the recognition is usually supported by environmental and situational evidence, i.e. it is likely for that person to be present at the particular time and place involved. There are, however, a few plants in the United States where access control is by voice ID, but these are experimental. Transaction ID by voice is rather common in securities, currency, and commodity exchanges, but only within a close community. Often, brokers on the stock exchange floor or in commodity pits, accept transfers of large sums with no more ID than voice. Currency exchanges use voice over phone lines for ID, but with the knowledge that the lines are part of a secure net and that only a few dealers, all well acquainted with each other's voices, have access to the net.

The use of voice ID in court is the subject of heated controversy.[1, 2] The device known as a *spectrograph* has been used in many court cases, and the verdicts have frequently been reversed on appeal. After numerous papers and lectures, the battle of the admissibility of expert testimony involving the *voiceprints,* as the spectrograms frequently are called, is far from settled. There are cases in which a spoken passage is used with the jury to decide whether it is the defendant speaking. In these cases, however, the recorded passage is but one element in the available evidence and is judged by the jury, or by a witness, not an expert.

CURRENT RESEARCH

A great deal of research is being done both in the United States and abroad in an effort to make voice ID practical. A method called *AUROS* is under development by E. Bunge in Hamburg.[3]

In this system, a sophisticated computer program is used, operating on utterances of ten seconds' duration. The work is aimed at fundamental research in speaker recognition, and AUROS is not proposed as even the forerunner of a commercial product. Correct recognition has been obtained in excess of 98 percent. The system seems to be as successful on unstructured text as it is on previously selected code words and suffers only a 1 percent degradation when operating over phone lines.

At the University of Washington, Holden, Cheung, and Gulut have worked on seeking out those features of speech that provide the greatest spread between inter- and intraspeaker variabilities.[4] These researchers are to be commended for deliberately avoiding prior research efforts and concentrating on new speech features.

The most practical work has been done at SRI International,[5] Menlo Park, California, and at Texas Instruments, Inc., Dallas.[6] The problem of using speaker recognition in a commercial environment has been addressed by these people.

All of the operative systems rely on a rather large sample, from six or seven words to ten or fifteen seconds of text. Common to all existing systems is a large, sophisticated computer system at the same location as the speaker. These are not acceptable conditions to the case of transaction ID for retail purchases.

THE SPOKEN NAME

It has often been suggested that a person could speak his name uniquely, just as he signs uniquely, thus providing a spoken signature for cashing a check or making a credit purchase. Unfortunately, the situation is not that simple. Spoken words are dynamic in nature and thus are not useful in prolonged and detailed study. In analyzing a graphic signature, the examiner can concentrate on certain parts at his own option, going back over any questionable strokes. Such detailed examination is not possible in a spoken name; the syllables are too volatile, too transient. Thus, if spoken words were to be analyzed, the analysis would have to be done electronically. In addition, certain words contain more acoustic information than others, and the choice of a name would not be wise. Consider, for example someone named T. Lee, uttering the name for analytical recognition by a bank teller. There is practically no usable data available in the name T. Lee. Even if the bank were willing to equip each teller station with a tape recorder and earphones, the phonetic comparison of voice expressions is not feasible. The spoken name is not a wise choice for a sample utterance.

VOICE AS IDENTIFICATION DATA

Unfortunately, there are cases in which the voice is the only available element that can provide ID. Due to the frequency of such instances, a great deal of research effort has been spent in trying to devise practical voice ID. As mentioned above, securities and currency exchanges are conducted almost entirely by phone; it is a closed group handling the data by a closed telephone circuit. Due to the extremely critical time value of the transactions, this group is unwilling to spend time with identifying code words or with communications that provide graphic records. These people have such high standards of ethics that it is rare that a mistaken identification occurs. Actually, it is more often that a mistake is made in the words spoken (price or quantity) than in the identity of the trading parties.

On the trading floor, most transactions are made in voice, supplemented by hand signals and visual recognition between the buyer and seller. If voice alone is the identifier, both parties usually confirm the transaction at the earliest opportunity.

The military often has no choice but to accept voice as identification. This presents a serious hazard, and the Department of Defense is vitally interested in voice ID research. Military voice communications are at best poor (either radio or wire) and subject to jamming by the enemy, thus presenting an extremely difficult problem in identification by voice. Currently, code words are used to identify the parties, but in the heat of battle these are cast aside. There is no way of telling the cost of mistaken identity in battle communications.

For typical retail transactions or in check cashing, voice seems an unlikely means of ID, because of its dependence on prior acquaintance. Usually, such transactions are between strangers, and although the parties are easily identified by role (one is customer and the other clerk), there is no reference available for the clerk to identify who the customer is. Again, some device would be needed to reduce the spoken words to easily compared signals. Such a device is not yet available, and it is unlikely that anything economically and operationally feasible will be available within the next ten years.

The conditions present at the point of transaction also mitigate against a good voice ID method. Background noises are not constant and are often of a high level. Space and wiring facilities present unique problems. Usually, the area where the customer and clerk come face-to-face, ready to conclude a transaction, is cramped and cluttered with other tools necessary to the trade, such as a cash register and a telephone. These locations are moved frequently or may even be portable, and the carrying of voice wires capable of providing broad-band, noise-free transmission is not feasible. In addition, the file necessary to provide data on today's mobile population would be excessively large. A central regional file would correct the file cost-space problem, but would introduce the need for long and expensive voice lines.

Finally, the customer himself is a stumbling block to voice ID in casual transactions. As mentioned above, certain words contain more acoustic data than others. An efficient system of voice ID makes use of these words. Yet, today's public would not tolerate speaking these seemingly foolish, unrelated words into a microphone. They might say their name and address, but these, while they contain useful textual data, may or may not be rich in phonetic data. Add to this the voice changes that come with emotional states, colds, chewing gum or candy, and the customer presents problems. Because of current consumer attitudes and technology, there must be alternatives to voice as transaction ID in the retail area.

It might surprise the reader that voice ID is claimed to be beyond the capability of today's computers while each of us practice it constantly in everyday life–and with a fair rate of success. First, the human brain, though slower in action than modern computers, is many times more capable than the finest computer man has yet devised. Even more important, humans consider more than just the voice in making identification: The text of what is heard is evaluated and assumptions (and errors) that are not permitted in a machine are made. People constantly update their reference files, perhaps with data that did not come (originally) from the voice. For example, a voice is heard at a cocktail party. Regardless of the background noise, we recognize the voice. Additional data input, however, was available: One, we expected that person would be there. Two, that person always gets excited at a party and projects a clearly identifiable "party voice" that is not similar to the normal voice. Three, the text of the overheard statement is a favorite subject of that person. No doubt there are other subtle inputs that are not even perceived as input but nevertheless affect the decision.

A machine, to be reliable, is restricted to those voice characteristics that have low intraspeaker variability (constant for one person) and have high interspeaker variability (widely different from person to person). Such features as pitch, for example, change readily in a person's voice. Pitch changes are intentional in the inflections a person applies in everyday speaking. Some pitch changes, also intentional, are habitual and almost impossible intentionally to prevent. The ability to use or suppress inflections varies from person to person and varies within one person, depending on circumstances. Emotions also affect voice pitch, beyond control. Thus, the astute listener considers these factors in endeavoring to identify the speaker. A machine, not knowing the emotional state, could not compensate for its effect on voice pitch. The physical condition of the speaker also noticeably affects voice volume. A weak, sick person has a soft voice–perhaps high in pitch, perhaps low, or maybe a whisper. Also, the passage of years has such a pronounced effect on a person's voice that voice quality is often taken into account in estimating a person's age.

There are, however, certain aspects of a voice that remain constant in a mature adult; features over which the speaker has no control. These are the qualities of a voice that result from the structure of the voice-producing organs of the upper throat and oronasal cavity (Fig. 15). While these features are useful in identification because they are constant within a person, they may also appear in a similar fashion in other persons. Frequently, brothers (or sisters) have voice characteristics so much alike that they are mistaken for each other. Generally, though, if the problem is to identify one person out of a small group, and all of the group

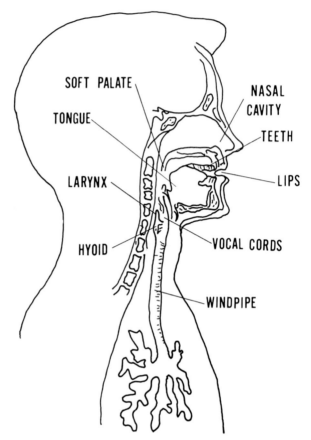

Figure 15. Sound produced by air passing the vocal cords is modified into words by the upper members of the oronasal tract. Some members are controllable, producing words. Others are fixed and tend to identify the speaker.

are available and willing to submit to a technical voice analysis, a clear identification can be made. Such an analysis involves the invariable resonances that are structurally fixed by the physical dimensions of the vocal tract.

Table II lists the relative usefulness of various voice features, with reference to discrimination, ease, and mimicry.

REQUIREMENTS OF A VOICE IDENTIFICATION SYSTEM

Since there are some features that can make voice ID a usable skill, and some that cannot be trusted, what are the requirements of a satisfactory voice ID system?

TABLE II

PERFORMANCE RANKING OF SOME SPEAKER
DISCRIMINATING MEASURES*

Measure	Level of Discrimination	Ease of Measurement	Difficulty of Mimicry
Waveform envelope	Good	Good	Fair
Voice pitch period	Good	Fair	Fair
Relative amplitude spectrum	Good	Good	Good
Vocal tract resonant frequencies	Good	Poor	Good

* From G. R. Doddington, Personal Identity Verification Using Voice, *Electro*
'76: May 1977. Courtesy of *Electro '76,* Boston, Massachusetts.

The samples, both unknown and reference, i.e. the sample taken
under known conditions, must meet the following criteria:

1. The voice must be easily separated from any noise introduced
   into the sample:
   a. Background (acoustic) noise present in the place the sam-
      ple was spoken.
   b. Transmission noise entered between microphone and rec-
      ord.
   c. Noise introduced in the playback machine or analyzer.
2. The voice must be recorded in an anechoic area, so there is no
   false reinforcement of certain frequencies.
3. The sample must contain words and phrases that occur frequently in the subject's normal speech, so that the subject
   has a habitual fashion of uttering the sample words.
4. The sample must be proven genuine, i.e. to have been made
   by the subject or suspect, under the prescribed conditions.
5. Both references and unknown samples should be made while
   the subject is in a similar state of health, rest (or fatigue),
   age, and emotional state.
6. Recording, transmission, and playback equipment must be
   of sufficient bandwidth to include all or nearly all of the
   frequencies present in the subject's voice.
7. Samples must be of sufficient duration and syllabic variety
   to demonstrate a representative variety of the subject's vocal
   capability.

The above criteria probably explain why voice ID is not here today. It is a demanding list for samples, even under ideal conditions. The public would not tolerate the physical facilities necessary to make the sample meet these criteria if ID were only for a retail purchase. The employee of a high-security area would likely accept the cumbersome environment required. In forensic situations, it seems unlikely that the unknown sample would meet the criteria, even though the reference samples could be so made.

In addition to these harsh limitations placed on sample taking, the analysis also has its criteria:

1. The defining features must be easily measured. The analyst may work from contour curves traced by a spectrograph or perhaps use a bar spectrograph. The cathode-ray tube can be used to provide data to the analyst. A photograph should be obtained if the CRT analysis is to be used in court. The analyst may want a computer program to do the work of wave analyzing. As yet there is no standard program or even standard hardware for voice analysis except the voiceprint. There are generally accepted tools (filters, CRTs, etc.), but each analyst is inclined to use them differently.

2. The measured characteristics must be consistent within and variable between speakers. This refers to the reliance on structurally affected features of the voice.

3. The measured characteristics must not be capable of disguise by the speaker (see above).

4. The analysis must be done by a competent professional if the identification is for court use.

ACCESS CONTROL BY VOICE

The only system now in day-to-day use that meets all of the sampling and analysis criteria is the one at Texas Instruments, Inc.[7, 8] It is used for security access control, not for forensic situations.

A similar system was developed at DataWest™ in Scottsdale, Arizona. The designers initially used conventional computers for processing the data. Surveying the transaction market, they felt that speed of use was needed and designed their own array processor in order to obtain quick analysis. The processor is complete and is now functioning. Texas Instruments, Inc., completed their model, and it has been in use for three years with constant improvements being applied. Its function is to screen employees as they enter the high-security computer complex, to ensure that only qualified people are allowed entrance (Fig. 16).

The employee steps into a soundproof acoustically treated chamber about twice as big as a telephone booth. He enters his employee number into a small ten-key keyboard, alerting the system to who he purports to be. A weight check is built into the floor to ensure that only one person is in the chamber at a time. The

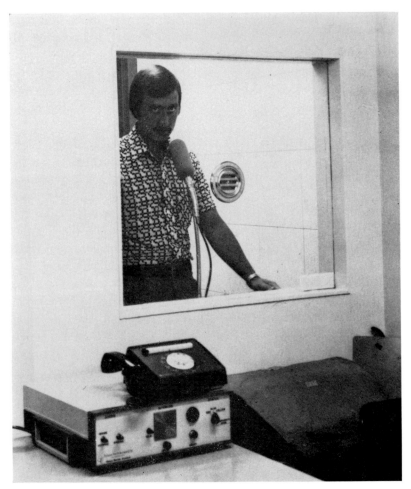

Figure 16. Employee in soundproof booth identifying himself by spoken words. (Photograph courtesy of Texas Instruments, Inc., Dallas, Texas.)

employee uses a microphone and loudspeaker for two-way communications with a proprietary computer system. The voice lines are broad band and noise free. Thus, the physical facilities satisfy 1, 2, and 6 of the first set of criteria. Number 4 is partially aided by the employee number and by the windows in the chamber.

The computer instructs (by recorded spoken statements) that the employee should state certain words. These words are in nonsense clusters of four each. The words are one-syllable words, and the groups and sequence are scrambled in a random (unpredictable) fashion. The randomness satisfies criterion 4. An imposter would be deterred from trying to use prerecorded utterances in the voice of a qualified employee, because the recorded words would not reasonably have the proper sequence or grouping. Also, the words are selected to satisfy criterion 3. All words, a collection of a total of sixteen for each employee, have previously been taken as a reference sample.

It is assumed that the employee is in a reasonably similar state of health, fatigue, and emotions since he is reporting for work. This covers criterion 6. Number 7 has been proven to be covered in the past few years' usage of the four-word grouping. The system offers up a second and third group (each four words) from the file of sixteen, if there seems to be some doubt as to the identification. Clear cases of accept are not bothered with a second time.

The analysis of the voice is done by a complex computer program that has been honed to a fine edge over the years of use. As expected, it relies principally on those resonances of structure that defy disguise and are least affected by colds and physical state.

For analysis, the voice spectrum from 300 to 2,700 Hz is divided into fourteen equally spaced channels. Each channel contains a complex of filters. The filter output is sampled every 10 msec and passed on to the processor. The processor then enhances the vocal tract resonances (constant regardless of the phonetics of the utterance) and suppresses the speaker-controllable characteristics. After normalizing and reduction to a bit pattern, the speaker's characteristics are matched against a reference matrix. The reference storage (disc) requires 9,408 bits for each speaker's file of sixteen one-syllable words.

The system now has over 200 employees on file. About 400

identifications are performed each day, with over 250,000 IDs having been performed to date. Usually, a person is identified on the first group of four words, but because of colds and changes in speech habits, an average of 1.3 groups (of four each) has been used. The false reject rate has been cut to 0.1 percent by fine tuning the system. Also, the system now goes through all sixteen words and then a complete retry before rejecting a person. Table III shows that the advantage in going beyond the second word group or phrase is rather slight, although certainly not negative. In a busy location, employees failing the second group could be asked to bypass the booth and be screened by more conventional ID methods.

At present, booth time is running 16.3 seconds for each employee entering. This can be reduced to an average of 14.3 seconds by allowing more than one person in the booth at a time. In this case, the weight platform is arranged to note the weight loss when the identified employee exits the booth. (The employee weights are filed with the voice characteristics.) It hardly seems worth the extra complexities and the likelihood of background noise during speaking, just to save two seconds.

Probably the biggest problem in the system is the time delay in performing the ID. This delay is an annoyance to the staff and can cause a queue at shift changes. With only four employees per minute, a queue of twenty employees would cost the last one in

TABLE III

VERIFICATION PERFORMANCE FOR A
SEQUENTIAL DECISION STRATEGY*

Percent of Speakers Accepted	True Speakers	Impostors
First phrase	75.24	0.24
Second phrase	18.60	0.08
Third phrase	4.87	0.11
Fourth phrase	0.95	0.13
On retry	0.28	0.26
Total	99.94	0.82

* From G. R. Dodding on, Speaker Verification for Entry Control, *Wescon:* September, 1975. Courtesy of *Wescon,* San Francisco.

line a five-minute wait. If the employees are in the habit of just flashing a badge at a guard, this could seem unnecessarily slow.

VOICEPRINTS

The situation in which voice ID is used in criminal identification is quite different from the above employee ID situation. An error rate of 1 or 2 percent can be accepted in employee screening, because of the high likelihood that the imposter would be recognized once in the plant. But to falsely identify an innocent man and accuse him of a crime allows no second opportunities for identification. In addition, employees are not only willing to be identified, but make every effort to be sure that the ID process succeeds. The reverse is usually true in a forensic situation. Thus, the use of voice ID in court has been strongly challenged as inadequate for the job.

The use of voiceprints for personal identification was first started by Lawrence G. Kersta. Kersta was originally at Bell Telephone Laboratories, but he soon left to establish his own company. He established a new company, Voiceprint Laboratories Corporation, in Somerville, New Jersey. The company's principal business was voice analysis and in training others in the skill. The analysis was centered around the Series 700 sound spectrograph, which was sold by Kersta.

In the early 1970s, Dr. Oscar Tosi, Department of Audiology and Speech Sciences at Michigan State University, and Lt. E. Nash, Michigan State Police, became strong proponents of voiceprints. These men have carried on Kersta's work for the past few years. Recently, they have analyzed voice spectrograms by computer, using the PDP-1140 and the CDC 6500 computers.[9]

The use of voiceprints to identify criminals is claimed to have been used in twenty-five states and in military and Canadian courts. This apparent success has caused some in the technology of voice analysis to point out that in all of the cases in which the voiceprint was successfully used, the expert was unopposed. Thus, the decision to admit the voice print was made by amateurs unacquainted with the technique. It is true that many cases have been reversed where the opposing attorney had his own expert in the appellate court.[10]

The thrust of the controversy seems to be that the two-week

training proposed by Dr. Tosi does not, in the opinion of the opponents, make the person an expert. Lawyers and judges are inclined to accept the experts,[11, 12] but most of the members of the professions involved in speech analysis do not support voiceprints as a means of identification.[1, 13] It could probably be said that voiceprints can successfully pick out which of a small group of people made a given recorded statement. The technique has been used to identify which member of a flight crew made a radio transmission. But, when a recorded statement could have been intentionally disguised or could have been made by any one of thousands of persons, the skill and technology are unable to perform successfully.

The method in making a voice spectrograph involves running a tape of the utterance many times over. Each time, a narrow band of the frequencies is examined to the exclusion of all other frequencies. Even though the tape is run at many times its recorded speed, it takes 80 seconds to complete a 2.5-second recording. In this period, 400 passes will have been made. The graphic record yields a "picture" in which time is the horizontal axis, frequency is vertical, and the intensity (blackness) is the amplitude of the voice. The machine may make contour spectograms (Fig. 17*B*) or bar spectograms (Fig. 17*A*).

The spectrogram is made on electrically sensitive paper wrapped around a drum. After the spectrograph has finished its run, this paper is removed and visually analyzed by someone expert in the skill. To compare two pictures is not easy, and the similarities or differences are not always obvious, even to the expert. At best, the interpretation is subjective and involves the opinion of the observer. With good software, today's computers could take much of the guesswork out of voice analysis, as indeed has been done at Texas Instruments, Inc.

STRESS ANALYSIS

Although not strictly an identification device, a new voice analyzer has recently come on the scene that does use modern electronic techniques. The device, the *stress evaluator,* uses recorded voice to detect "stress tremor," as evidenced by a low-frequency modulation of the voice. The common name for the machine is *PSE.* As in the voiceprint method, the device relies on a compe-

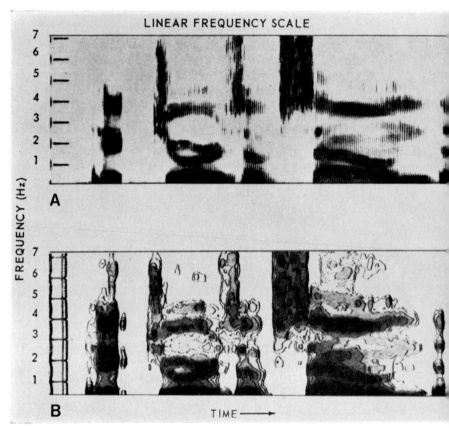

Figure 17. A bar voiceprint *(a)* and *(b)* a contour voiceprint of the same utterance. (Photograph courtesy of the *Journal of the Acoustical Society of America,* New York, New York.)

tent operator-interpreter. The machine is used much like a polygraph (lie detector), in that questions are addressed to the subject under test. Unlike the polygraph, though, his replies are recorded on tape, and the tape is later analyzed by the machine. The examiner's skill is in the selection and phrasing of the questions. The analyzer can only sense the stress as shown in the uttered response, since the only input is through the microphone. Thus, while a question might cause the subject an initial shock (which a polygraph would record) it is only the stress of answering that is detected by the machine. The device is too new to have established a track record, but it is being frequently used, and a cadre of competent operators is being developed. It is not a good tool for identification. Even though one could certainly ask the subject "What is your name?" the use of an alias might go undetected. The question of name is usually reserved for a standard reference question, i.e. a question that the subject realizes has a known answer and also that the answer is known to the operator. Stress analyzers are available from a number of companies, including Communications Control Systems, Inc., New York City; Dektor Corporation in Springfield, Virginia; and Law Enforcement Associates, Inc., Belleville, New Jersey.

TAPE RECORDING EQUIPMENT

When recording voice for possible use as an identification aid, it is important to obtain high-quality tapes. The average cassette machine is not adequate, although it certainly is sufficient if only the text is important. For voiceprint analysis, the recorder should be capable of frequencies up to 9,000 Hz. Not only is this beyond most off-the-shelf recorders, but the small portable microphones that come with these recorders are more limited than the recorder itself. Battery-operated recorders are to be avoided, unless portability is essential, in which case fresh batteries must be used. Tape speed as well as amplification varies with the condition of the battery.

If the sample tape has been poorly recorded, a good laboratory playback can be operated to compensate for some of the degradation. These machines usually have variable tape speed, broadband (flat) amplifiers, and enough output to permit filtering. Often, it is necessary to filter out 60-Hz hum that is in the original recording. For PSE recordings, it is necessary to have both recorder and playback capable of low frequencies–down to 20 cycles.

Even the best equipment cannot overcome a bad recording environment.[14]A background noise such as a motor or a pump may be sufficiently constant that it can be filtered out in playback, but such broad-band noise as a crowd or auto traffic cannot be eliminated, except at the source. Radio or TV audio can be disturbing and should be avoided. It is not possible to filter out aircraft or vehicle noise when radio transmissions are the recorded source.

Since such circuits usually use noise-cancelling microphones, similar microphones should be used when subsequently recording reference tapes for identification.

SUMMARY

Although voice identification is frequently used in closed business groups or in social situations, its use is not yet perfected for security access control and certainly not for forensic situations. The voiceprint method has been vigorously challenged and has not subdued the challengers. However, the new electronic techniques have shown that the future should bring voice ID within ten or fifteen years. This hope is the result of a successful computerized voice access control system at Texas Instruments. This realization could be the work of DataWest of Scottsdale, Arizona,[15] Threshold Technology of Delvan, New Jersey; or Texas Instruments, Inc.'s continuing studies.

REFERENCES

1. Bolt, R. H., Copper, F. S., David, E. E., Jr., Denes, P. B., Pickett, J. M., and Stevens, K. N.: Speaker identification by speech spectrograms: some further observations. *J Acoust Soc Am, 54:*531-534, 1977.

2. Tosi, O., Oyer, H., Lashbrook, W., Pedry, C., Nichol, J., and Nash, E.: Experiment on voice identification. *J Acoust Soc Am, 51:*2030-2043, 1972.

3. Bunge, E.: Automatic speaker recognition by computers. *Proceedings of the Conference on Pattern Recognition and Image Processing.* Troy, New York, IEEE, 1977.

4. Holden, A. D. C., Cheung, J. Y., and Gulut, Y. K.: The role of idiosyncracies in linguistic stressing cues and accurate format analysis in speaker identification. *Proceedings of the Carnahan Conference on Crime Countermeasures.* Lexington, Kentucky, University of Kentucky, May, 1976.

5. Becker, R. W., Clarks, F. R., Poza, F., and Young, J. R.: *A Semi-Automatic Speaker Recognition System.* SRI Project 1363. Menlo Park, California, SRI, 1972.

6. Hair, G. D. and Rekieta, T. W.: *Speaker Identification Report.* Final report. Texas Instruments, Inc., Dallas, Aug., 1972.

7. Doddington, G. R.: Personal identity verification using voice. *Electro '76,* Paper 22-4, New York, New York, IEEE, 1976.

8. Doddington, G. R.: Speaker verification for entry control. *Wescon,* Sept., 1975. Paper 31-3, New York, New York, IEEE, 1975.

9. Tosi, O.: Personal communication with the author, May, 1978.

10. Hollien, H.: *Status report of voiceprint identification in the U. S.* Read before The International Conference on Crime Countermeasures, Science, and Engineering, Oxford, England, July, 1977.

11. Lachey, R. D.: Evidence-voiceprints: The value of spectrographic analysis. *Georgia State Bar Journal, 9(2):*241, 1972.

12. Kogan, J. D.: *Voiceprints: Witchcraft or Scientific Evidence?* Read before the American Academy of Forensic Sciences Annual Meeting, St. Louis, Feb., 1978.

13. Hollien, H. and McGlone, R. E.: An evaluation of voiceprint technique of speaker identification. *Proceedings Carnahan Conference on Crime Countermeasures,* Lexington, Kentucky, University of Kentucky, May, 1976.

14. Fitzgerald, J. T. and Hollien, H.: *Speech enhancement techniques for crime lab use.* Read before The International Conference on Crime Counter-Measures, Science and Engineering, Oxford, England, July, 1977.

15. Long, P. J.: Personal communication with the author. Mar., 1978.

Chapter 7

SIGNATURES AND HANDWRITING

THE PERSONAL SIGNATURE, though now considered the typical business identifier, is a fairly recent development. We are still living in what future historians may call "the paper age." Prior to the advent of cheap paper and the printing press, the masses were illiterate, and few could even sign their name. Even when business first was conducted on paper, signatures and signed documents remained the province of the wealthy elite. Not until the nineteenth century did it become acceptable for the average person to enter into business commitments. Still, the signature was a record of commitment, not a means of identification. Only in the twentieth century did the signature take on the meaning of identification. Even today, there are far more court cases where the signature has been involved as evidence of commitment than cases in which it was considered as identification. Most cases in civil law are between two people who were known and identified to each other at the time the agreement was drawn up, and the litigation is then over what the signers agreed to, not who the signers were.

Just as a lawyer is required to interpret a contract, an expert is needed to interpret a signature. It is more difficult to compare signatures than to compare fingerprints. The original patterns from which matching fingerprints are made are identical beyond the control of the identifyee. But, two signatures by the same identifyee can be made in different ways. The difference may be intentional, perhaps may be an effort at disguise, or can be influenced by conditions beyond the signer's control. Some people, endeavoring to distort their signature, will reverse the slant, or will cramp the signature into a short block. External influences, such as gloves, a cold location, perspiring hands, a strange pen, or emotional excitement, affect the signature. If these conditions are known to the expert, they can be taken into account when the signature is being analyzed, thus making the task of signature comparison less difficult. At best, identification by signature is not a simple

100

job and should be done by experts who have the training and, above all, the tools to do the job.

There are over a thousand people in the United States offering services as document examiners. As such, they claim expertise in analyzing paper, rubber stamps, pen marks, etc., as well as handwriting. It is generally recognized that only about two hundred of these are totally qualified, and most of these are employed by government crime laboratories. Regrettably, there is no licensing procedure for this profession, and each expert seems to have his own set of credentials. Membership in one of the professional associations is probably the best way of qualifying an expert.

PERSONALITY ANALYSIS THROUGH SIGNATURES

Certainly, any act a person voluntarily performs, writing, talking, walking, or simply shaking hands, reflects to some degree his own personality. It is unlikely that a bold, aggressive person would have a tiny, carefully executed signature.[1] One is equally unlikely to find a meek person with a signature similar to the one John Hancock affixed to the Declaration of Independence. The busy executive who signs dozens of items per day does not waste time on neat, vertical slant signatures; he dashes off a sloppy scrawl, usually with a strong right slant. Beyond these broad generalities, though, there is little in a signature that relates to the personal traits of the signer; and even these obvious generalities have many exceptions.

There is even less correlation between personality and text handwriting. In a signature, a person is intentionally conveying himself as a person. In textual handwriting, a meaning of the words is to be conveyed, and the only reason for moving the pen is to facilitate that conveyance. Also, as handwriting is taught, a signature is created. Again, then, while some few personality pointers may exist in a signature, they certainly do not exist to a significant degree in written text.

The majority of those who practice the art of reading character (or personality) by handwriting are students of one of the many schools of the subject. The dominant school is the International Graphoanalysis Society, in Chicago. This school offers courses in the subject by correspondence and holds regular meetings of those who practice. The title *certified graphoanalyst* is conferred by the school on those who complete the course. Although the term *graphologist* is more general, it also refers to character analysis by handwriting. Neither term refers to the expert examiner who establishes identity by comparing handwritten material. Of course, training and experience in the study of samples of handwriting, regardless of the intent, is of benefit, but to ascribe personality characteristics to the loops, slope, and gaps is not for the serious examiner. His only responsibility is the identification of the author of the specimen.

The belief that the writer's personality traits can be deduced from handwriting, and, in particular, signatures, is quite prevalent. Certainly, it seems harmless, as long as the analysis is confined to parlor games. But when handwriting analysis is applied to employment qualifications or in the selection for advancement within a group, it can be damaging. In an effort to put to rest the value of graphology, a test was conducted, comparing the opinion of handwriting analysts with the findings of a recognized personality inventory. A population of forty-eight students prepared handwriting samples. The tests were conducted with great caution to avoid bias. Not only were the ratings of the graphoanalysts compared with those of the personality inventory, but after the ratings, each student was asked to evaluate the analyst's findings. For statistical purity, each was also asked to evaluate a rating sheet (chosen at random) that was not his.

The report concludes that "no agreement was found between personality profiles as determined by the Edwards Personality Inventory and the assessments by professional Graphoanalysts."

This study has been reported in a number of publications[2, 3, 4] and is available as a reprint from the Department of Psychology of Wright State University in Dayton, Ohio.

HANDWRITING CHARACTERISTICS

A person's handwriting is not without certain recognizable traits, nor can these traits can be disguised successfully. A handwriting sample can be analyzed and shown to contain features that the writer consistently imparts to all of his writing. This is especially true when the comparison specimens contain enough script to permit many iterations of certain telltale letters. It is also advantageous to have the examples written over a long period of time at one sitting, so the writer relaxes and concentrates on the text, thus forgetting to disguise the natural features he may have successfully masked in the first few lines.[5]

In criminal cases, the questioned writing is usually one involving a criminal act and, thus, was most likely written while the writer was excited and under emotional stress. An example taken for comparison should also be taken under stress and, thus, should be a fair document for comparison. Since age also affects one's handwriting, the exemplar should also be taken in the same life period as the questioned writing. This is not to say that "old" exemplars cannot be used. They may be all that is available. But a personal letter written when the suspect was a young man, and perhaps prior to his criminal career, is not as good for comparison as one taken shortly after the crime under similar conditions of stress and emotion.[6]

DISGUISED SIGNATURES AND FORGERIES

False signatures are not always forgeries. The criminal who endeavors to copy the signature of another person in an effort to represent himself as that other person is a true forger. But there are many cases where a signature is made that is actually a nonsignature. The bad-check files are full of signatures of "Ima Thief," "U. R. Had," and "George Q. Washington," etc. One wonders how these checks are accepted, but it happens every day. These are seldom prosecuted as forgeries, even though they could probably be traced to the maker. In executing such nonsignatures, the writer usually makes no effort at disguise, and the characteristic slant, height ratios, and gaps are clearly his own. In a true forgery, the signer tries to create a duplicate that will pass undetected and is thus concentrating on the characteristic features of his victim. Often, forgers copy the signature upside down in a deliberate attempt to eliminate their own natural features from the resultant signature. In cases of good forgeries, the forger's own features may not be apparent except to the expert, or even then, not at all.

There are three general categories of forgeries.[6] The *simple forgery* is one in which the imposter makes no effort to mimic his victim's handwriting–but only knows his name. The second category, of which there are many subtypes, is the *simulated signature*. In this case, the forger tries to make his work an exact copy of an available true reference signature of his victim. Two subtypes are identified as copies made with the reference present or copies made from the memory of the reference. Usually the one made slowly and artistically with the reference near at hand is the best forgery. The ones made from memory may be hurried, as in the presence of a witness, and the forger wants it to appear that he is signing his own name. Unless there has been ample opportunity to practice many times and to study and compare the results, the memorized simulation forgery shows characteristics of the forger and rather few of the victim's handwriting traits. The third forgery category is the *traced forgery*. Such a signature looks much like the original, but has indications of a slow, deliberate hand motion.[8] To the amateur, the form likeness makes the tracing resemble the original. To the expert, the details give it away.

In the field of check cashing, the memorized simulated forgery is becoming the only way the forger can succeed. Most clerks and tellers have either been taught or have learned from experience to ask the party presenting the check to sign in their presence. This forces the criminal to make a memorized simulation. The true signer has no hesitation about a second signature. If requested, he will even further identify himself by writing his address and phone number on the check. A forger, even though he may know the address and phone number of his victim, will hesitate to provide all that handwriting, which could be used as evidence against him in court. Some forgers try to present a check they have previously signed and then use the first signature as a reference in creating the second signature; a copy simulation in addition to perhaps a traced one. This, of course, is not possible if the first signature is on the face of the check and the second one on the back. The clerk may suggest that the second signature be placed upside down. Then, only the signature that was made in the clerk's presence is used for identification, even though it is upside down.

At the secure plant entrance, where a signature is required for entry, the simple forgery is frequently used. In truth, the signature log is kept primarily so that management can know who was in the plant at the time of some unusual occurrence. Seldom is any effort made at matching a signature against a reference. In most cases, a typewritten name suffices. However, since most people are hesitant to forge a name, the log serves as a deterrent to the small-time operator. Meddling in the affairs of a secure plant does not appeal to the forger; he wants cash. Thus, the log appears adequate in satisfying a regulation as to the degree of security and identification employed.

The traced forgery is used where the forger has the opportunity of preparing his document ahead of time. In mail fraud or on items for deposit, the traced forgery is often used. Usually, the signature is traced once lightly in pencil, then traced a second time in ink, usually in ball-point pen. An expert detects the "line quality" in such a tracing because the pen will have made deep and rather uniform indentations. The true signature usually shows a wide variation in indentation depth, due to the varying speeds of pen motion.[5] It is regrettable that pen motion is not more easily recognized by the expert, because it is one feature that is difficult for the forger to copy. In the days of the dip pen, the speed of the pen tip could be estimated by the breadth of line and by the density of the ink. In an effort to make a more perfect writing instrument, the manufacturers have created the ball-point pen, which lays down a nearly consistent line, regardless of speed. It does, however, leave an indented groove that its predecessors did not show. This groove has meaning to the trained expert.

DEVICES TO AID SIGNATURE COMPARISON

The handwriting expert, as well as the fingerprint expert, has a laboratory full of tools to aid him in his work. In addition, as there are now fingerprint devices for the teller window, there are also available signature analysis aides to assist the teller. In the laboratory is a binocular microscope of ×10 to ×15 power. (For field use, a ×4 or ×5 power magnifier is used.) A camera, either an instant-developing or a press camera, should be used to record signatures on a one-to-one scale. For handwriting that has been overstamped or for traced forgeries, it may be necessary to dissolve inks (always after photographs have been taken). Inks may yield to water, alcohol, benzene, or acetone, depending on the base of the ink. For viewing ball-point indentations, a halogen lamp of variable intensity should be used at a low angle. To photograph this, the camera should have a ground-glass focusing aid. Work with the indentation must be done before any solvents are used, because the solvents may react with the sizing of the paper and obliterate the groove. For some cases, where ink separation is important, as in overstamps or signatures over a printed area, ultraviolet and infrared light sources may be necessary.[6] A well-equipped signature-analysis laboratory is not as expensive as a fingerprint laboratory and is essential to forensic work. The Department of Justice has briefly outlined the equipment it recommends for a modern crime laboratory.[7]

At the cashier's window, signatures must be examined for an immediate decision.[8] This is unlike the forensic situation, and until recently, has not had the benefit of devices to assist in the decision. Even today, most of the devices only help gather data and do not help in the comparison with file signatures.

Originally, signature cards were kept in tub or drawer files at the bank where the customer did his business. If a check was presented by the customer at a different bank, his identity had to be established by some means other than his signature. His mother's maiden name or the date and amount of his last deposit were often used, because these elements could be transmitted over the telephone, but his signature could not. More often, someone employed by the bank who knew the customer would vouch for his identity.

Nearly a century ago, the Telautograph was invented for transmitting handwriting. Soon it was perfected to transmit signatures, and it is used for that today (Fig. 18). To transmit via the Telautograph, though, it is necessary that the signature be written on the machine. This means that a person presenting a check at a remote bank signs on the machine, and then an officer at the home bank compares the received signature with the card on file. But, the cashier taking the responsibility of accepting the check is at the wrong end of the wire. Thus, the signature comparison is made by the drawee bank, but the action is taken by the holder bank. This way the person making the identification is not the one taking the risk.

Figure 18. A modern telautograph for transmitting handwritten signatures and data. (Photograph courtesy of Telautograph Corporation, Los Angeles.)

There are now facsimile machines for transmitting signatures that were previously made, as on signature cards.[9] This transmission takes two to five minutes, depending on the format used. The reversal of responsibility does not take place in this instance, because the file signature can be sent to the holder bank and the comparison made there. Standard facsimile equipment is adequate for this purpose, since the judgment is made on the form of the signature rather than on detail. One system specifically designed for signature comparison, uses a strip of paper only 3¾ inches wide and transmits the signature in eleven seconds. The system, called Signa-Fax®, is manufactured by Alden Electronic and Impulse Recording Equipment Co., in Westborough, Mass.

Standard Oil of Indiana is now experimenting with a signature retrieval system that provides a signature from file for each credit card transaction.[10] The system, though, is not for ID at the time of the sale. Rather, it retrieves and prints the stored signature on the monthly statement as proof of sale. The customer then knows who signed the slip. When this system goes into effect, the oil company will stop returning the sales ticket to the customer with the monthly statement. As yet, the storage medium is not good enough to provide matchable signatures to detect forgeries, but it is adequate to identify which member of the family signed the sales ticket.

With the increased use of paperless CRT terminals, the transmission of signatures by video is becoming more popular. Not all of these television terminals adapt themselves to the smooth curved lines of a cursive handwritten signature; some are limited to a coarse dot pattern that displays only preformatted capital letters and numerals. Also, some systems do not transmit video signature patterns because of the telephone line limitations. In an effort to overcome these deficiencies, the display can be made to show the signature at four times its size, using the regular dot pattern of the screen. While this provides more detail, it is difficult for the clerk to scale the change down to actual size. Additionally, the fluorescent green usually found on CRT screens is difficult to compare with an ink signature on a check. Two video systems are now in use for transmitting signatures. In New York at Emigrant Savings Bank, IBM has installed their Instagraphic® signature validation system (Fig. 19). The Commonwealth National Bank in Dallas uses the device made by Signature Technology, Inc. In both of these systems, the signatures are stored magnetically in the data base memory, along with the account statistics, and transmitted to the teller location upon request.

As an alternate to transmitting the signature from a central reference to the teller window where the customer stands, some have suggested that the customer bring his reference with him. In fact, this is done by the signature panel on most credit cards and check-cashing cards. The risk, of course, is that the signature panel is an open invitation to the forger. To defeat this, there have been many systems to scramble or chemically treat the reference signature so it does not appear as a true signature. Most popular is the use of ultraviolet ink. The signature is applied using a pen with UV ink or through UV tracing paper and is thus invisible. Each teller is provided with a so-called black light, which makes the signature glow. Of course, such lights are easy to obtain if the forger is serious, but the system has been effective in deterring amateurs and is in use in thousands of banks.

A system called Opticode® scrambles the signature so it appears as a smudge rather than a signature.[11] The scrambling lens con-

Figure 19. Signature transmitted to CRT along with file data for identifying bank customer. (Photograph courtesy of Emigrant Savings Bank, New York, New York.)

sists of hundreds of tiny lenslets pressed together in a common frame. A similar lens is supplied to each teller station, so that the smudges can be descrambled. In this method, the clear signature is scrambled and printed on each check when the magnetic numbers and depositor's name are printed. (The ink may

Figure 20. Scrambled and unscrambled handwritten words. Scrambling makes forgery nearly impossible. (Line drawing courtesy of Opticode, Inc., New Orleans, Louisiana.)

or may not be magnetic.) An example of the scrambling is shown in Figure 20.

When the check is presented, the teller inserts it in a viewer and compares the descrambled smudge with the signature on the bottom line. This provides the teller with the reference for comparison without any wires to central or without having to leave the window to go to the card file. Yet, the forger has no model to copy. It is, of course, true, that a forger could obtain a descrambling lens and thus do his work. However, each bank has a different lens system and keeps close custody over the teller units. It would take a clever crook to break the system. For the supermarket, the system has its problems, because of the necessity of having a descrambler for each bank. There is also the concern of counterfeit checks with nonsignatures scrambled on them, but with valid account numbers. Like any antiforgery system, there are hurdles to be cleared. At present, Opticode of New Orleans has the system in use at the Boston Five Cent Savings Bank. The signature in this case is put in the passbook, which seems an ideal use of the system. Similar optical scramblers have appeared on the market from RCA, Le Febure, Baush & Lomb and Signasure.[12] There are powerful economic reasons favoring any system that has the customer bring the reference to the place of transaction. Only the technique needs to be solved.

COMPUTER-AIDED SIGNATURE ANALYSIS

The advent of the computer has provided business with a wide range of previously inconceivable capabilities. One of the most recent is the ability to identify people. Computer analysis of voice, facial features, body geometry, and memorized codes are all discussed elsewhere in this book. The single most promising identity feature is the computer recognition of signatures.

A signature is not given or even taught; it is cultivated. It can be changed at will, although it generally remains the same throughout adult life. Thus, the signature satisfies that seemingly ridiculous but prevalent wish to be able to identify oneself or not, as the circumstances seem to warrant. The signature is accepted, and always has been, in business transactions. For secure access control, the signature is also accepted and much used. In forensics while it is not well suited because of the ease with which it can be disguised, it is often used as the only evidence available. Usually, in forensics, pages of handwriting are used. During a long session of writing, the disguises fall away or are so inconsistent that they can be cast out, leaving the true characteristics available for analysis.

Recognition of the static signature is a form comparison done by observing the questioned and reference signatures. Such a comparison is made by the retail clerk for nearly every credit card purchase (often inadequately) and by the cashier or teller for check cashing. These people have little training in this skill and often make mistakes. People must not be blamed categorically for poor signature recognition. Some people are *form blind,* a term applied to a type of dyslexia or stephosymbolia. These people have difficulty with graphic representation, including reading, while having average or above-average intellect in other areas. Because signature comparison is often inadequately done, business has sought to strengthen the identification process with photo cards and memorized passwords. Recently, work has been done in the use of electronic devices to perform signature comparison. There were earlier attempts, and no doubt others are currently at work, but the references listed at the end of this chapter constitute most of the available data on the subject.

The first exhaustive study of handwriting analysis by computer was by Eden of M.I.T.[13, 14] During the early 1960s, in collaboration with others and a formidable array of computer power, he tackled the problem of reading handwritten cursive English script. Although his work was not directed particularly at signatures, much of it is applicable.

The approach was to break down each cursive block, not into letters but into strokes. The strokes then could be reassembled into letters. Eden tried to make his analysis writer independent, assuming the writers were all taught writing in this country. There are certain basic elements such as bar, hook, and loop, etc. Most of these can be positioned in right-for-left mirror reflection and can occur either high, middle, or low in respect to the writing line. This method allows each letter of the alphabet to be represented by as few as two strokes (*c, e,* upper case *L*) or as many as ten (upper case *M*).

Since Eden's effort was to analyze words and not signatures, it was necessary to verify the resulting letter group against a dictionary of 10,000 common English words. Admittedly, verifying a signature would be considerably easier. At that time, the computer recognition of signatures appeared to be commercially less rewarding than replacing secretaries. The automatic teller machines and unattended cash vendors were yet to be envisioned. Eden conducted a few experiments using specific strokes of identified individuals in graphic comparisons and achieved much improved results. His work was to be the foundation of later efforts at signature recognition at the University of Maryland.

Leon Harmon[15, 16, 17] at Bell Telephone Laboratories studied the cursive script of general handwriting in 1960. He classified the letters of the alphabet in an effort to devise a method of machine reading handwritten pages. Although he intended to invent a system that would recognize letters, independent of the writer, much of the work can be adapted to signature classification and recognition. He looked at letters statistically with respect to two heights above the line, two below, cusps (pen reversals producing points), closures, retrograde strokes (pen motion in part from right to left), and special marks (dots, crosses, and slashes). The input to the system was dynamic, i.e. the subject wrote on a telewriter tablet and the features were extracted on-line. Yet, the analysis was independent of pen speed, thus essentially static recognition. Harmon started his work on an IBM 704 computer and has continued with more recent machines as they became available.

More pointedly directed toward signature analysis is the study of Roger N. Nagel at the University of Maryland.[18, 19] Nagel's work was done on bank checks, and thus he dealt with real signatures. He used Eden's model as a guide to extract stroke features rather than discrete characters from his samples. This is possible because the intent was to recognize the signature as a form, not read and understand the words (or characters) in it. The stroke features were then statistically classified and the signature was reduced to a formula that could be tabulated and filed. It is relatively easy for a computer to look up a signature in such a reference file, given the formula being sought. Since his system was intended to work on bank checks, the entire check was digitized and the signature portion recognized in the digitized form as standing out from the printed data, background, and other written material. The system allowed for near-matching signatures, which are typical of signatures in the real world. It is quite likely that traced forgeries or even good freehand forgeries would have slipped through this system. For locating forgeries on checks as they pass through the processing system this work has merit, but it is not suited to the teller window.

Opticode is also developing a method of analyzing signatures for forgery as they pass through the processor. The system is much like the optical descrambling that Opticode developed for the unit at the teller station, but the descrambled signature and the endorsement are further processed electronically. By performing a Fourier transform (optically) on each image, minor differences are eliminated, and then signatures are matched electronically. This method also includes a scrambled image of the account number, so that the smudge could not be lifted off and transferred to an account of a different number or to a different bank. With the danger of counterfeit checks thus reduced, this method may find acceptance. Obviously, such preprinted reference information of any type would not fit the credit card systems, unless the preprint were on the plastic card so that it could be transferred to the sales slip by imprint. Even if such a transfer could be made and were still not available to the forger, the credit cards are used at so many millions of end points that security would be almost impossible to maintain. The sophisticated signature comparison systems are usable on checks only.

A study was made at the University of Missouri at Columbia, using computer techniques to examine the overall form of the signature.[20] This is perhaps more closely related to the method used by clerks and tellers in making the quick decision on a check signature. Form recognition overlooks the strokes or letters and even bypasses the syllable appearance in multisyllable names. The fine details of cusps and lifts are omitted from the analysis. Thus it would seem that a reasonably good forgery would pass the form test proposed in this study.

The testing at Columbia was done by only four subjects, one genuine and three imposters, but with no attempt at simulated signatures. The three had no knowledge of the true signature of the one, except the spelling. Also, only the first name *Loren* was used, and the true signature was formed without a pen lift after the initial *L*. The other signers had to make the *L* and the *o* intersect so that the scannner could follow the line as a continuous image. While this was a minor technological problem, it placed a constraint on the forgers.

The report makes a good case for the recognition of word forms, but considerably more detail is required to separate a forgery from a true signature. It appears that the Fourier transform, as proposed here, is more suited to pattern or form recognition in medical, scientific, or geographic photographs, where there is no attempt at disguise. This study reported a high rate of definition between the true signer and the others (98.8 percent, using thirty descriptors). However, this is deceptive, because there was no attempt at deceit. The questioned signatures were all simple forgeries, i.e. the correct spelling in the forger's own handwriting. Perhaps the use of hundreds of descriptors focused on only certain parts of the signature would yield a definition that would recognize forgers.

In general, it appears that the examination of static signature images, either by humans or by machine, does not effectively isolate the forger, unless a lengthy examination is involved. Often, this examination must take place in the laboratory where the tools of chemistry, optics, photography, and recently, computers can be used. This is not the typical courtesy booth in the supermarket or even at the bank teller's window; yet, the signature is the most popular and least offensive of all ID methods in use today.

SIGNATURE DYNAMICS AS A MEANS OF IDENTIFICATION

There appears to be great promise in identifying a person by the pen motion used in signing. This is not a new concept, except in detail. Many cashiers know that only the competent forger risks signing a false name in the presence of a cashier. This is because the forger cannot imitate the speed and flourish of the true signer and still create a similar-appearing signature. It is interesting to note that the paying cashier has no knowledge of the true signer's usual pen motion, either. If the forger could in any way speed through the signature with an appearance of genuineness and produce a good graphic image, the payer would never know the difference. Such skilled forgery is seldom seen. If the teller could be equipped with some information on the true signer's dynamics, forgers would have to seek another method of livelihood.

Consider, for example, the simplest of tools, a pressure tablet[21] or a pen tip that is sensitive to contact with the paper and a magnetic-stripe ID card. For further simplification, consider an identifyee, a bank customer, named Millie Stiltti.[22] Mrs. Stiltti has a definite habitual pattern in which she crosses her *t*'s and dots her *i*'s (Fig. 21). She is asked to sign her name three times when she opens her account. The timing of these crosses and dots is recorded by the tablet and digitally encoded on the magnetic stripe of a plastic check-cashing card, which is given to her as an ID card.

Each time Ms. Stiltti comes to the bank to cash a check, she is asked to endorse the check in the presence of the teller. To do this, she places the check on a tablet similar to the one she used when she made the three reference signatures and signs with her usual signature. Before signing, the plastic card was presented to the teller, and the teller inserted it in the card slot associated with the tablet. As she signs, the timing of the pen lifts and strikes is sensed by the tablet and compared with that previously encoded on the card. If the timing matches reasonably closely and the signatures look alike, the check is accepted.

The data encoded on the card shows that in signing her first name, Millie, she habitually dots the first *i* immediately after com-

Figure 21. The name *Millie Stiltti* has many return strokes that are isolated in time from the cursive part of the signature. The timing of these returns is unique and known only to the proper signer.

pleting the first name, then dots the second *i*. Then, after a brief pause of about one-fourth second, she starts the last name. After the completion of the last letter, she dots that *i* and, passing from right to left, crosses the last two *t*'s, the first *t*, then the left (first) *i* is dotted in the last name. This is an habitual sequence that even she cannot describe. To someone casually watching her sign, the events occur too fast to be observed. But, by repeated observation or aided by a slow-motion video tape, the timing could be detected. However, the tablet or wired pen can accurately time each lift and each strike as the signature is made. Ms. Stiltti's time pattern is shown in Figure 22, along with the signature. The pattern shows that after two and one-half seconds of continuous contact, the pen is lifted and makes two strikes within the next quarter

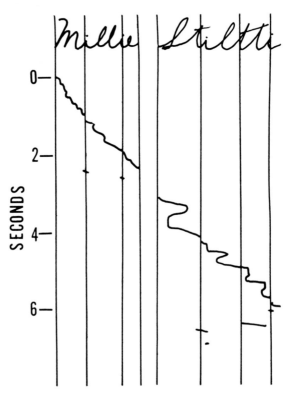

Figure 22. Below the signature is the time diagram, showing when the strokes were made in the course of a normal signature.

second. Then, after a quarter-second halt, another long, continuous stroke is sensed. This is followed immediately by a lift and a strike, a pause, a long strike, a short strike, a pause, and the last strike, a short one. From first contact to last, six and one-half seconds has elapsed.

This signature pattern could be represented by seven pairs of digits. The first of each pair indicates a one-second interval, and the second digit of each pair represents the number of pen contacts during that second. This simple bit stream would be put on Ms. Stiltti's magnetic stripe as an indicator of her dynamic signature pattern in its simplest form. The forger has no way of knowing the speed or sequence of dots and crosses involved with the signature. Thus, he cannot duplicate the dynamics pattern when he signs.

At the teller window, if the timing pattern generated matches the one recorded on the card, the signature is accepted, and the comparator flashes a green light. If it is a mismatch, the signature has deviated too far from the record, and the teller is alerted to ask some questions. Simple signature dynamics may have caught a forger, without any judgment or training required of either the teller or the customer.

With more sophisticated tablets, much more data can be gathered, and a higher accuracy could be obtained from the same effort by customer and teller. An FA-to-FR ratio per thousand of 2/50/1,000 should be possible with even the simple tablet described above, assuming an average active bank window.

The important feature of using the dynamics of a signature is that the forger has no way of knowing the speed or pen-lift sequence of his victim's signature. Once the ink is dry, no telltale signs call out whether the *t* is crossed after the first name, or after the entire cursive part has been written. No one knows how long it takes a person to write his name or how long he pauses between the first and the last names. Frequently, the signer himself does not know and cannot answer these questions.

Today's technology permits measuring pen position as close as 1/2,000 inch. Time can be easily measured to a billionth of a second. Measurements of a signature to this fine a degree would be ridiculous, but a position accuracy of 1/50 inch and time intervals of 1/20 second would clearly define the true signer. Some compensation would have to be made for the day-to-day differences in signature, but here again, the technology available can account for anticipated changes that the forger could not forecast.

So plausible is the field of signature dynamics for ID that it is the subject of many research efforts. The Bank of America has a project in time-related pen-tip pressure; IBM is currently testing and has patents issued on signature pen acceleration; and Citibank, through its subsidiary, Transaction Technology, Inc., is studying dynamics. In the past, 3M, Sylvania™, Sandia Corp., and Rockwell International have had projects in signature dynamics. Two of the major research institutions, SRI International and Battelle Institute of Switzerland, have devices for reading signature motion. Of course, numerous small laboratories are also working on machines.

Of all the projects going on, the IBM effort has the best chance to succeed. They have an issued patent[23] that is written to deter challenge from any but the most sincere attorneys. It has fifty-six drawing figures and eighty columns of text, much of it sophisticated mathematics. Although only thirty claims were allowed, they, too, are worded in a difficult mixture of legal patent jargon and mathematical symbolism.

Prior to the issuance of the patent, a paper was submitted to the *IBM Journal of Research and Development,* describing the method.[24] (It was not published until a year later; meanwhile, the patent was issued.) Then, the patentee delivered a paper describing the method at a technical seminar a few months later.[25] Thus, the boundaries of the IBM preserve are boldly, if vaguely, drawn.

Summarizing the published information on the IBM device is difficult, since it purports to cover such a broad area. To the casual observer, the IBM method seems to center on two issues, i.e. pen-tip acceleration and regional cross-correlation. The detection process uses a wired pen with semiconductor strain gauges to measure X and Y components of pen motion and a pen-tip pressure gauge to measure contact with the paper. (In later tests, this was replaced with a tablet switch.) The vertical or contact measurement (usually called Z-axis measurement) is merely an on-off measurement, whereas the X and Y are analog measurements. The Z measurement and a clock measure total time of signature. Signature time alone is a discriminating factor, especially if pen-contact time is the only measure. While a person may vary the gaps between cursive segments, once the pen starts making a trace, the time to the next pen lift is usually consistent. IBM reports start to finish consistency as close as 10 msec in successive signatures. If gaps were deleted, this would probably be closer. The IBM screening technique first compares the total time (five to ten seconds) of the sample signature with the reference signatures previously provided. A variation of over 20 percent is cause for rejection. If the signature passes this test, the vastly more sophisticated test of pen acceleration takes place.

For reducing the pen motion signals to digitized form, an IBM System 7 samples the strain gauges at 5-msec intervals. This data is then passed on to an IBM 370/145. The 370 performs the comparison of sample accelerations with the reference file using a PL/I correlation program. The typical system response is ten seconds from completion of the signature. This is an indication of the complexity of the computation required. IBM now acknowledges that this is more data and more computation than is needed, by at least five times.

There are some interesting features of the first IBM test. The seventy subjects gave five reference signatures each, at the time of enrollment and only twice as many in test signatures up to the time of the writing of the report. This is hardly a fair sample. A ratio of five references to 100 or 200 test signatures would seem more meaningful. A group of 287 forgery attempts were included in the test, over and above the other test signatures. The "forgers" were allowed to witness their victims in the act of signing and were given graphic samples from which to practice. Some of the forgers were also closely acquainted with the project and thus unusually cognizant of how to succeed. When the experiment was limited to one test signature and one reference signature, 20 percent of the 695 true signers were rejected, and 1.4 percent of the 287 forgers were accepted. By allowing three tries at the test signature, the rejection rate dropped to below 3 percent, and the forgeries accepted rose to 2 percent. The forgers were skilled in the operation of the machine and had a good knowledge of their victim's hand writing. This is hardly a real-life condition.

These results are definitely encouraging. Rated roughly in the scale of Chapter 4, it would be an approximate FA-to-FR per thousand of 2/17/1,000. It is especially heartening when it is known that some of the rejects and perhaps some of the accepted forgeries were the result of malfunction. Also, the reject rate was undoubtedly raised by requiring the use of a bulky, wired pen. More testing and new design is continuing at the IBM Thomas J. Watson Research Center in Yorktown Heights, New York.

IBM has been most generous with some of their basic findings. They have pointed out that the feedback loop from what the eye sees at the pen tip to a reaction of the muscles that change the pen-tip motion is 200 msec. Yet, in making a signature, the typical motion increments are of only 30 to 100 msec duration. The act of signing, then, is not a feedback function, but is a direct brain memory function. Yet, a forgery must be a feedback function. It has long been known that a signature, even most handwriting, is a ballistic motion, i.e. the result of practice. The way a person walks, picks up the telephone, or swings a golf club, are all ballistic motions. Such motion is not to be confused with the involuntary reflex, which is not practiced but is inborn. The ballistic motion of a signature is certainly learned and not a conscious reaction to an observed pen trace. Thus, IBM felt a sensing of signature dynamics should be a conclusive way of identifying people.

The introductory observations by the IBM research team also shows insight not seen in most laboratories. They point out that previous work on signatures by pattern recognition experts did not fully recognize the work of the competent forger. Signatures, unlike most pattern recognition targets, are constantly challenged by an intelligent external force endeavoring to simulate a signature pattern to near perfection. Also, unlike the visual pattern recognition problem, images do not need to be classified, but the real have to be differentiated from the forged. Furthermore, in signature analysis, for all but forensics, the signer's identity is known. For these observations alone, the IBM experiment is outstanding. If subsequent experimental efforts are not buried in statistical overkill (which is not only unreal, but unaffordable), the Yorktown laboratory may have the solution to the identification problem in business transactions. A recent research report[26] indicates a Type I error (FR) of 1.7 percent and a Type II error (FA) of 0.4 percent.

The best of the early work on computer signature dynamics was done at GTE Sylvania Inc., at Mountain View, California in the late 1960s.[27] The testing was done on a Sylvania data tablet, which extracts X and Y positional coordinates of the pen tip. These can be related in sequence with the previous points, and thus velocity and acceleration rates can be computed. It was discovered, as it was in the IBM experiment six years later, that there is very little intelligence in handwriting dynamics above 10 Hz. Thus, although the tablet had a high basic resolution, filters were used to block out all above 15 Hz.[28] A total of forty measurements were compared, involving pen contact, velocity, and acceleration. As in the first IBM test, the sample was small. It proved, however, that the forty measurements permitted a clear decision between forger and true signer, even when the forger was well informed about the victim's signing habits and the nature of the test. Subsequent experiments found that fifteen measurements were adequate for a clear definition.

The similarity of the IBM patent and the Sylvania patent point up that (1) the United States patent system has some unfortunate features in its makeup and (2) that signature dynamics in some form will probably be the future method of transaction ID.

Another group of independent and nonassociated investigators seem to have hit on a method involving the time or motion relationship of pen-tip pressure. The tablet or pen for such a method is much simpler, and the system can even be made to work with the writer's own pen. Veripen[TM], Inc., of New York has devised a pen transducer that produces an analog signal proportional to the pressure on the ball-point of the pen. This signal is related to time from a zero start and analyzed digitally throughout the signature.

The identifyee enrolls with six signatures, the first being rejected as a warm-up. These are averaged by pressure and time and filed for reference. The test signature is then recorded on the same or an identical tablet and compared electronically to the reference. An oscilloscope trace shows the similarity of the signatures, and, in fact, it might be expected that a trained person could achieve near-perfect results by simply a visual comparison on a dual-trace oscilloscope. But to take the human being out of the decision, the trace is digitized and compared in a minicomputer. In a test conducted by the MITRE Corporation for the United States Air Force,[29] the Veripen unit showed a Type I error rate of 6.8 percent and a Type II error rate of 3.2 percent. This would be an FA-to-FR factor of 32/68/1,000. The Veripen method is now commercially available under the name Signac® from Sentracon™ Systems in Westwood, Massachusetts.[30] A photograph of the desk and pen is shown in Figure 23. Similar work has been done at the National Research Development Corporation in London. The British unit is available on the market and is under test by Esso® as a secure access control device.

At San Jose State University (California) another pen-tip pressure device has been developed. It uses a graphic strip chart recorder and requires a trained expert to interpret the charts.[31] Patents involving the same Z axis versus time principle have been issued to Burroughs Corporation, Mosler Safe, and others.

The men at these major laboratories and no doubt numerous others who have not patented their efforts all use horizontal and vertical components of the pen motion. SRI was the first, and their pen is commercially available through Xebec™ Corp., in Sunnyvale, California. However, the Xebec rights are limited to computer data input. To use the pen for signature analysis, one would have to deal separately with SRI. Numerous improvements on the first pen (1959) have been made and patented by SRI. Most of the methods involve tracking the pen position with a plotting or telewriter tablet. By computations, these positional locations can be converted into velocity or acceleration. According to the previously cited work at IBM, acceleration is a definitive feature in a person's signature. However, there seems to be more than enough data in velocities, as found by H. W. Crane at SRI[32, 33] and J. W. Dyche at Sylvania.[28] The Sandia device[34] takes the velocity and acceleration data directly from the pen without reference to position. At SRI, the data was also from the pen.

Figure 23. Sentracon relies on pen-tip pressure and timing to delineate the unique features of a signature. Device extracting this data is shown. (Photograph courtesy of Sentracon Systems, Inc. Westwood, Massachusetts.)

The pens in all of the above cases presented problems. A person is not used to signing with a bulky instrument with a wire attached. In most cases, the pen was critical as to orientation, thus requiring attention to a sign saying "This side up," or in one case, the pen had a triangular body. Those using tablets to record X and Y positions were further involved with expensive and delicate tablets. Of course, these were all research devices and not designed for use by the general public. Still, even with sample populations of a few hundred, and even though they were laboratory employees, some rejection was indicated because of the equipment.

Some researchers took a more simplistic approach and dealt only with velocity. Usually, this involved a velocity type data sensor and a minimum of processing. Such devices have been announced by the Battelle Institute (Switzerland), Wim Van Leer (Israel), and the author. The Van Leer device[35] is a moving ribbon of paper that condenses the pen image by having the paper move from left to right. If the paper speed is the same for reference signature and sample signature, the resulting image remains similar. Figure 24 shows a signature symbol, which might be produced in the Van Leer device using a paper speed of ½ inch per second.

Both Battelle[36] and the author sense the velocities electronically. The Battelle instrument accepts X and Y data and even senses the pen motions when the pen is in the air. The forger, of course, has no way of detecting the flourishes of the true signer if they are not during the period the pen is in contact with the paper. The Warfel device[37] may act on X and Y velocities or on X (vertical) alone. By using only X data, the cramping of signature length that is common in most signatures where the panel or box specified on the form is short, is not permitted to distort the data. Most people cramp the length but permit the vertical height to go unaltered when signing in a close area.[38] Although the Warfel device does not record the motion of the pen during pen lifts, the clock continues to run. Thus, the duration of the lifts, a significant and secret part of every signature, are part of the record.

Figure 24. The Van Leer method reduces the signature to a unique scramble by moving the paper under the pen.

In addition to the above attempts to make signature-analyzing devices, at least two efforts have been made at evaluating the field.[39, 40] Each month, there seem to be new patents. To date, most signature-dynamic ID devices have been too sophisticated and represent overkill. The basic advantage of signature dynamics is that the forger has no record, no data, and no sample from which to work. It is not necessary to take thousands of bytes of data, when the elements are unknown to the forger. In fact, one should not take more data than is needed and thus hold some in reserve. A wisely chosen ten or twenty bytes reduce the odds of success by forgery to an acceptable minimum for everyday business transactions.

A quantity of this value can be taken from a grid at twenty lines per inch. Also, it has been found that almost no useful data exists in handwriting above the level of 10 Hz. Certainly the signal-to-noise ratio above 20 is vastly more difficult to deal with, since most paper noise is above 20 Hz. Thus, the emphasis should not be on great amounts of data. Another feature of signatures that is not usually considered is that the signer is not in a hurry. He will wait a few seconds for an answer. A fast computer is not needed to evaluate and compare.

With all of these advantages, it would seem that signature dynamics are a natural task for a simple tablet and a microprocessor. It is proposed that simple capacity or acoustic tablets be used to extract the data and that the first and the last seconds of the signature be sampled for local analysis at the teller window or supermarket courtesy desk. For most low-dollar checks, these two elements of information could be compared against similar data on a magnetic stripe card carried by the patron. By using first and last segments, the timing error due to slow signatures would not be great, because the data was taken near a well-identified time marker. Such a comparison would be simple enough for the slowest microprocessor, especially if the data were limited to vertical velocity. For higher dollar amounts, where the clerk was suspicious, or perhaps just on random chance, the entire signature could be transmitted to a regional data center and checked by more complex electronics. Thus, the dynamics would occasionally be used to check at the regional center and at the point of transaction simultaneously. If the criminal was able to cheat at the regional center, perhaps through an accomplice, the local location would trap him. Such a dual method would minimize the risk of wiretap fraud or manipulation at the central data bank.

Truly, signature dynamics, if implemented on a simple, unsophisticated basis, could be the dominant method of transaction ID in the immediate future.

REFERENCES

1. Zweigenhaft, R. L. and Marlowe, D.: Signature size: Studies in expressive movement. *J Consult Clin Psychol, 40(3):* 1973.
2. Vestwig, R. E., Santee, A. H., and Moss, M. K.: Validity and student acceptance of a graphoanalytic approach to personality. *J Pers Assess, 40:* 1977.
3. Vestwig, R. E., Santee, A. H., and Moss, M. K.: Validity and student acceptance of a graphoanalytic approach to personality. *Hum Behav, 6(8):* 1977.
4. Vestwig, R. E., Santee, A. H., and Moss, M. K.: Validity and student acceptance of a graphoanalytic approach to personality. *Identification News, 27(8):* 1977.
5. Pascoe, T.: Questioned Documents. Lecture, San Jose State University, San Jose, California, Mar., 1978.
6. Conway, J. V. P.: *Evidential Documents.* Springfield, Thomas, 1959.
7. Steinberg, H. L.: *Standard Reference Collections of Forensic Science Materials: Status and Needs.* Washington, D. C., U. S. Dept. of Justice—LEAA, 1977.
8. Thompson, P. C.: Forgery detection through handwriting analysis. *Bank Administration, 51(2):* 1975.
9. Facsimile machines verify signature in seconds. *Savings and Loan News, 98(8):* 1977.
10. Eaton, W.: Personal communication with the author, Feb., 1978.
11. Warfel, G. H.: *ID: Where Are We Now?* Palm Springs, California, I.D. Code Industries, 1977.
12. Kahn, D.: *The Code Breakers: The Story of Secret Writing.* New York, Macmillan, 1967.
13. Eden, M.: Structures of language and its mathematical aspects. *Proceedings of the Symposium in Applied Mathematics,* Providence, Rhode Island, Am Math, 1961, Vol. 12.
14. Eden, M. and Kolers, P. A. (Eds.): *Recognizing Patterns,* Cambridge, MIT Pr, 1968.
15. Harmon, L. D.: Machine Reading of Handwritten Script. Internal document, Holmdel, New Jersey, Bell Telephone Laboratories, May, 1959.

16. Harmon, L. D.: Computer Simulation of a System for Reading Cursive Script. Internal document, Holmdel, New Jersey, Bell Telephone Laboratories, July, 1960.
17. Harmon, L. D.: Computer Simulation of a System for Reading Cursive Script, Modification and Experiment II. Internal document, Holmdel, New Jersey, Bell Telephone Laboratories, May, 1961.
18. Nagel, R. N.: *Computer Screening of Handwritten Signatures: A Proposal.* College Park, Maryland, University of Maryland, 1973.
19. Nagel, R. N.: *Computer Detection of Freehand Forgeries.* Unpublished dissertation, College Park, Maryland, University of Maryland, 1976.
20. Sprouse, L. V., Zuefle, D. L., and Harlow, C. A.: *Automatic Verification System from Human Signature Images.* Columbia, Missouri, University of Missouri, 1973.
21. Danna, S. R.: U. S. Pat. No. 3,489,911. Signature Identification Instrument. (Filed Oct., 1965; issued Nov., 1969.)
22. Warfel, G. H.: Input security in electronic funds transfer system. *Comp Con '75.* New York, New York, IEEE, 1975.
23. Herbst, N. M. and Morrissey, J. H.: U. S. Pat. No. 3,983,353. Signature Verification Method and Apparatus. (Filed Mar., 1975; issued Sept., 1976.)
24. Herbst, N. M. and Liu, C. N.: Automatic signature verification based on accelermometry. *IBM J Res Dev, 21*(3): 1977.
25. Herbst, N. M. and Liu, C. N.: Automatic signature verification by means of acceleration patterns. *Proceedings of Conference of Pattern Recognition and Image Processing,* Troy, New York, IEEE, 1977.
26. Liu, C. N., Herbst, N. M., and Anthony, N. J.: *Automatic Signature Verification: System Description and Field Test Results.* Research report. Yorktown Heights, New York, IBM, June, 1968.
27. Dyche, J. W.: U. S. Pat. No. 3,699,517. Handwriting Authentication Technique. (Filed Sept., 1970; issued Oct., 1972.)
28. Dyche, J. W.: Positive personal identification by handwriting. *Proceedings of the Carnahan Conference on Electronic Crime Countermeasures,* Lexington, Kentucky, University of Kentucky, 1976.
29. Haberman, W., and Fejfar, A.: Automatic identification of personnel through speaker and signature verification: System description and testing. *Proceedings of the Carnahan Conference on Crime Countermeasures,* Lexington, Kentucky, University of Kentucky, 1976.
30. Davis, J. K.: Ultimate security in personal identification. *Security World, 12*(8): 1975.
31. Chang, M. A. and Huang, G. C.: *A Technological Approach to Signature Analysis.* Read before the American Academy of Forensic Sciences Annual Meeting, St. Louis, Feb., 1978.

32. Crane, H. W.: Personal communication with the author, 1973.
33. Crane, H. W.: U. S. Pat. No. 4040010-11-12. (Filed Nov., 1975; Aug., 1976; and Apr., 1976. Issued Aug., 1977.)
34. EerNisse, E. P., Land, C. E., and Snelling, J. B.: Piezeelectric sensor pen for dynamic signature verification. *Proceedings of the International Electron Devices Meeting,* New York, New York, IEEE, 1977.
35. Van Leer, W.: Personal communication with the author, Feb., 1977.
36. Vermat-Guad, J.: Personal communication with the author, May, 1978.
37. Warfel, G. H.: U. S. Pat. No. 3,955,178. Signature authentication system. (Filed Oct., 1974; issued May, 1976.)
38. Morton, S. E. and Truman, V. R.: *A Comparison of Scrawled to Normal Signatures.* Read before the American Academy of Forensic Sciences Annual Meeting, St. Louis, Feb., 1978.
39. Werner, C. L. and Zimmerman, K. P.: SIRSYS: A research facility for handwritten signature analysis. *Proceedings of the Carnahan Conference on Crime Countermeasures,* Lexington, Kentucky, University of Kentucky, May, 1978.
40. Zimmerman, K.: Real time handwritten signature recognition. *Proceedings of the West Coast Computer Faire,* San Jose, California, Mar., 1978.

Chapter 8

IDENTIFICATION CARDS

To a great many people, ID and plastic cards are inseparably associated. In most instances, the phrase "May I see your ID?" means "Show me a card." Although plastic cards have many purposes, identification is usually involved with the card. Most often the card is convenient, i.e. it conveys a right or enables a transaction, and the identification feature merely assures that the card is in the proper hands. The driver's license, for example, is the permission for a certain person to operate a motor vehicle. The printed photograph, fingerprint, personal description, and signature prevent someone else from exercising that permission. The credit card, with its raised letters, imprints the account number on the sales slip so that it may be processed without error. This is purely an operational function in the accounting system. But to assure that the card is in the hands of the person who is responsible for paying the monthly bill, added identification (usually a signature, or perhaps a photo) is on the card.

CLASSIFICATION OF CARDS

There are hundreds of millions of cards circulating in the United States. They range from cheap paper library cards to engraved and gold-lettered membership cards. Nearly all carry identifying data. There are, of course, billions of other cards, usually heavy paper stock that are admission tickets. These are transferable and thus carry no ID information. They are not personal cards.

The myriads of personal cards can be conveniently separated into machine-readable or nonmachine-readable cards. Most machine-readable cards can also function without being machine read, but are still classified as machine-readable cards. It is also true that many machine-readable cards carry additional data that must be read manually, but any ID card that can be at all machine read will be considered as a machine-readable card. In Table IV, cards that are popular in the United States today are listed according to their data features.

TABLE IV

Machine-Readable Information	Manually Readable Information
Magnetic spots	Printed numbers
Magnetic areas	Typed
Metallic slugs	Preprinted
Magnetic stripe	Embossed
(One to five tracks)	Tipped
Infrared bars	Not tipped
Ultraviolet spots	Photographs
Optical (visual band) spots	Black and white
Holes (Hollerith type)	Scrambled
Self-punch	Color
Prepunched	Engraved photos
Embossed (raised) bars	Signature
OCR printed fonts	Printed name
Proximity cards	Embossed name
Embossed characters	Tipped
	Not tipped

MAGNETIC SPOTS

Cards with magnetic spots are formed as a sandwich of two outside layers of polyvinyl chloride (PVC) plastic bonded to a center core of barium ferrite. The construction may show the three layers when examined at the edge, or the magnetic barium ferrite may be an insert in a center core of PVC. In the latter case, the layers are not visible at the edge. Sometimes, as the card ages, this insert or window may show as outline cracks on the surface of the outer plastic layers. The card can be printed with a logo or instructions over the entire area before assembly and may have a signature panel. The encoding is in the form of spots of polarized magnetic fields electrically induced into the barium ferrite. A pattern of from ten to one hundred spots provides many thousands of individual codes.

The cards are encoded by positioning the barium ferrite panel beneath a cluster of electromagnets. These magnets have sharply focused fields. As a momentary high current (usually a capacitor discharge) is passed through the coil of the electromagnet, an instantaneous but strong magnetic field is created. This permanently magnetizes a spot of $\frac{1}{8}$ to $\frac{1}{4}$ inch in diameter in the barium ferrite. The patterns of spots can be made to represent a number in binary code. Once encoded, the cards hold their magnetism indefinitely, although they can be erased and re-encoded. The usual magnetic fields encountered in a normal environment do not alter the card. To use the card, the person inserts it in a slot, and the magnetic spots are sensed either by reed switches or coils in the reader. Some readers have mechanical toggles that are attracted by the magnetic spots and position themselves like tumblers in a lock. There are many patents issued for cards of this type, some of them now in the public domain.

MAGNETIC AREAS

A patent was issued to Walter Barney[1] for a card similar to the one described, except that the barium ferrite panel was magnetized in large, irregular areas. The card was claimed to be hard to duplicate (counterfeit), yet easy to read. It was one of the dozens of patents issued to Barney in the field of magnetic ID cards.

METALLIC SLUGS

In the 1950s, some plastic cards were made with metallic pieces about ¼ × ¼ inch buried in the center core. These carried no magnetic field of their own, and thus the card appeared to be a simple plastic card. The reader, however, had a cluster of magnetic fields in it. When the card was inserted in the reader slot, these fields were affected by the slugs in the card. If the slugs had been so placed that the field was altered in a pattern the reader was planned to recognize, the card was considered valid; otherwise, it was rejected. Some other readers used electric fields (low-power radio frequencies) and thus operated on copper or aluminum (nonmagnetic) slugs. Encoding of each of these cards relies on hand placement of the slugs before the card is laminated. Of course, the code is permanent.

A new and unique card using metallic rods is now on the market. A recently discovered magnetic reaction, the *Wiegand effect,* allows a credit card to be permanently encoded and read without power.

The Wiegand card uses individual wires for each bit of intelligence. The wires are smaller in diameter than a needle, and less than one-half inch long. By a patented process, these rods are hardened on the outside shell and develop two layers of magnetic properties, one in the core and one in the shell. These rods are then buried in a plastic ID card of standard dimensions. By passing the card through a magnetic field, these embedded rods switch states and generate a strong instantaneous magnetic field. This field produces a sharp electronic pulse in the sensor coil integral with the magnet. It can be truthfully said that the pulse generation requires no batteries or electric supply. However, since batteries (or a 115-V AC source) are required to operate the analysis circuit, this is not a big plus. The Wiegand method, though, is totally new and represents innovation. With increased research, it could be a good ID card; however, it is unlikely it will ever replace the magnetic stripe. For high-security access control, it could be an excellent card.

MAGNETIC STRIPE

The most important machine-readable card in service today is the "mag stripe." It has a history all its own and has a dominant position in the card business because it is the chosen standard of the bank credit card industry.

History

The American Bankers Association (ABA) saw the need for a machine-readable card as soon as the credit card movement began. At that time, there was little technology that could offer a durable reading method. Chase Manhattan Bank had done a survey and concluded that by attaching a magnetic recording tape to a plastic card, a good machine-readable card would result. The airlines had also experimented with magnetic stripe cards for ticketing. The airlines, however, had a different objective. They planned to use the magnetic stripe as a source to transfer data to the ticket. The blank ticket was made with an unencoded stripe; then, by pressing the blank stripe against the encoded stripe on the card, a data transfer was to be affected. The proposed transfer did not succeed, but it is interesting to note that the airlines selected magnetics because of the natural tendency toward transferability. In an effort to study the situation, the ABA issued a call to interested parties to have a competitive demonstration of available technologies, including the magnetic stripe. In the end, the magnetic stripe was chosen as the standard of bank credit cards. The original specification called for two encoded tracks, one for airline ticketing and one for bank credit card use. There are now three tracks.

Standardization

In the complex of data that is on the stripe, there is an area in the bank credit card track (track two), called *discretionary* data, on which a bank may put any information it chooses. All other coding is dictated by the standard. This area of approximately seventeen numeric characters is quite adequate for ID, but must function with other uses, such as auxiliary account numbers, loan information, etc. The area is set aside for the bank to use as it pleases, but personal ID information was one of the goals when the track format was defined.

Shortly after the banks adopted the stripe, the electronics research laboratories began developing equipment to implement the stripe into point-of-sale equipment. Standards were written and exist today at the American National Standards Institute[2] and at the International Standards Organization.[3]

The mag stripe card, although standardized by the banks for credit cards, has been used in parking lot tickets, mass transportation tickets, and for plant entry control. It seems likely that it will be around in many uses, taking advantage of the extensive development financed by the banks. The mag stripe has one outstanding flaw that makes it a poor choice for the credit card, yet it is a good method for cards carrying a lower value: Magnetics are changeable and copyable. The reason for magnetic tapes and disks in computers is because they can be erased and rewritten. Shortly after the stripe was selected by the ABA Committee, it was pointed out that data could easily be transferred from one card to another by a simple electronic skimmer.[4] This reduced the security of the card, but the banks did not alter their position.

Security Methods

Recent developments have been offered to make the stripe more difficult to alter, but have not been accepted as standard or even used in the marketplace by the banks.

One method with the tradename Watermark®, by EMIDATA/ Malco in Garrison, Maryland, proposes to seal an unalterable pattern in the magnetic material. This can be seen by the naked eye on close examination and certainly leaves a definite magnetic pattern that can be seen as slant (45°) striations in the stripe. The format can be coded in a pattern put on at the time the stripe is applied to the plastic.[5] Another method, offered by 3M of St. Paul, is application of two layers of different magnetic material in a sandwich. By making one layer of hard or high-coercivity material and another layer of soft or low-coercivity material, it is impossible to alter the hard stripe without also altering the soft stripe.[6] At the time of manufacture, however, before the two layers are combined onto the card, certain fixed data is encoded on the hard layer. Then after assembly, perhaps even at the time of issue, the soft layer is encoded in the normal fashion. It can be arranged that the discretionary area of the soft layer is encoded with some feature that was previously read from the hard layer. The two layers are thus permanently related, and any attempt to alter the soft layer could be detected. It would also be possible to read the two layers with different head angles. This seems a simple system (though not quite as simple as described above), but it has not yet received the approval of the ABA.

At first, the banks were reluctant to admit that the mag stripe card should carry personal ID information. They felt that there was so much marketing advantage in the credit card that they could afford to absorb the fraud losses. Then, in 1975, the bank-sponsored report on security was issued by the MITRE Corporation.[7] This work clearly admits to a serious exposure to fraud through the magnetic stripe and proposes methods of prevention. The prime proposal, a cryptographic check digit, fell on deaf ears when announced, as well it should have, as the cure was not fitting to the disease.

Thus far, none of the proposed methods of preventing fraud have involved personal identification. The signature panel, while it meets the legal requirement, has not solved the problem. The PIN number, even when encrypted and put on the mag stripe, is not the answer. The banks must find some means of linking the person to the card, in a fashion that is fast, cheap, and above all, acceptable to the public.[8]

As a Data Card

The magnetic stripe, as a source of data, has become an excellent device. The industry took a stand, established a goal, and induced the technical community to produce the tools needed. There are a number of readers on the market today with only one moving part, and that part is the card itself. To transfer data from the card to the system, the customer merely passes the stripe briskly through the slot in the reader. Clever slot design and software make this reader tolerant of slow motion (down to a point), shaky fingers, warped cards, worn edges, and the dozens of errors that can occur when the public is operating a machine. Telephone dialer cards using a slot reader are now available. The slot reader could be used for library cards, hospital accounting, and security access control–anywhere where fraud is not critical. With the 3M dual-coercivity stripe, even high-risk uses could be implemented. (As yet, the 3M stripe is limited to relative low data content.)

The data content of the standard card is 79 alpha-numeric characters on track one (210 bits per inch) and 40 numeric characters on track two (75 bits per inch).[2] Recently, track three has been added at the same data capacity as track one, yielding a total capacity of approximately 200 characters. Some nonstandard stripes have as many as five tracks, for a total of 200 numeric characters at a very low data density. These are used in the automatic teller machines. Vertel, Inc. of Clifton, New Jersey, has announced a data card patterned after the bank cards (but larger) with nearly all of the surface covered with magnetic material. It has a total capacity of over 1,000 characters.

As noted above, the magnetic stripe card is fundamentally a data carrier.[9] Unless the data is information about the cardholder, it is not an ID card. Because of the ease of exchanging data from one card to another, it would not be a *secure* ID card. Thus, while the magnetic stripe card may become an excellent ID card, it currently is not that. This is evident in that of the 500 million magnetic stripe cards that have been issued, less that one-tenth of 1 percent of the stripes are read.

Coding and Decoding

The mag stripe card is unique among machine-readable cards, in that mechanical motion is necessary to the reading process. All other cards (except the Wiegand) can be read in a static condition, but it is essential to the mag stripe that the stripe move in respect to the reading head to induce the decoding voltages. Many other cards use motion to economize on the reading sensor, i.e. one sensor may pass over a column of many encoded elements, but only the stripe is critical in speed because of the emf generated in the pickup head. The other cards using motion for passing elements past a fixed head usually use a clock pattern. This is discussed later.

The Aiken code used in the stripe relies on sharp reversals of magnetic flux to generate the data. It is called a *self-clocking code,* because there is a predetermined flux reversal for every bit space. If the flux has reversed between two of these adjacent clock reversals, the bit is called one; otherwise, it is zero. Figure 25 shows the pulse pattern. While it seems that the banks chose a sophisticated and unsecure method of encoding their cards, the impetus given by the early selection of a standard has been fruitful in research, and the mag stripe may yet emerge as a much-used encoding method. The recent development of dual coercivity and the Watermark make this even more probable. If the same pressure

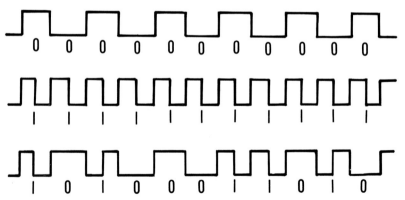

Figure 25. The magnetic stripe coding is a two-phase Aiken coding with a self-clocking feature. The card must be in motion to be successfully read.

could be brought to bear on a personal ID method, the bank credit card could someday create a cashless society.

INFRARED ENCODED CARDS

Contrary to the efforts of the ABA, one bank, Citibank of New York, went its own way. This bank, the second largest in the world, voted in favor of the magnetic stripe card as a standard and then reversed itself in favor of infrared reading. The Citicard®, a product of Citibank's research subsidiary, Transaction Technology, Inc., has a fixed code put in at the time of manufacture.[10] Because of this, it cannot be given any personal ID characteristics that are machine read. It is also necessary to go through an on-line data exchange, switching from the pre-encoded number to the later-applied embossed number, which is the account number. This cumbersome and expensive procedure is executed every time the card is used.

For all of its complexity, the bank has pushed the Citicard nationwide. It has held the method proprietary and the technique of making the card is secret. To do this, the bank has built its own factories, using its own employees; licensing has been minimized and complete control has been kept over the card, the reader, and the manufacturing process.

Where the mag stripe is readily alterable, the Citicard is virtually fraudproof. To change a code requires a knowledge and a skill found in few people outside of the Citicard factory. And, since all transactions are on-line, even a good counterfeit would soon be noticed.

The principle of the IR card (and Citicard is not the only one) involves passing a low-level infrared light through the card and detecting a pattern of shadows. The shadow pattern can be read much like punched holes can be read, by optical sensors. Yet, to the unaided eye, the card seems uniformly opaque. The standard 3/100-inch thickness of PVC is transparent to infrared (IR) light. To encode the card, the core stock (also PVC) is printed with a bar code that is different for every card. The patterns of some IR cards are shown in Figure 26. Because the card is so transparent to IR, the light source can be small, light-emitting diodes. These solid-state devices are like the red bars in the characters on the average pocket calculator, except they are shaped into a small, round disc. They have an infinite life and generate no heat and thus are ideally suited for an IR source. The sensors are also solid-state devices operating at peak efficiency in the IR range. Because the components are so cheap, many readers have a pair (source and sensor) for each code spot, thus using a full array. Solid-state electronics interpret the shadow pattern of this array into a manageable number code.

Some readers, including Citicard's (Fig. 3), use a linear array reader that reads only one line of code at a time. To minimize timing problems, a clock track is printed with a code element in every line. This code element issues the command "Read" as it passes its sensor and thus times the acquisition of the line of data. The clock track can be seen down the center of the Citicard and the Lawrence card in Figure 26. The Toye card shows a clock track down the lower margin.

Infrared cards not only have a security not seen in magnetic cards, but a stability superior to any other card. The low level of light, the use of light outside the visible spectrum, and the buried coding make the IR card paramount. It is regrettable that the coding has to be frozen at the time of lamination, so that machine-readable personal ID traits cannot be added.

Recent work has shown that it may be possible to make an IR card that is postencodable. By printing a full field of code elements in every card during the manufacturing phase, it could then be possible to eliminate certain code elements at a later time by a strong electromagnetic field. The process would be costly and might reduce the life of the card because of the side effects of the strong field, but research may make it feasible to postencode cards that were made in blank form. Not only would this allow the card to be encoded with personal ID characteristics that could be machine read, but it would allow a decrementable card such as a ten-ride commuter ticket to be machine read.

To expand the code possibilities of the IR card, a patent has recently been issued for encoding the shadow elements in different levels of translucency.[11] The technique is termed *multiple trans-*

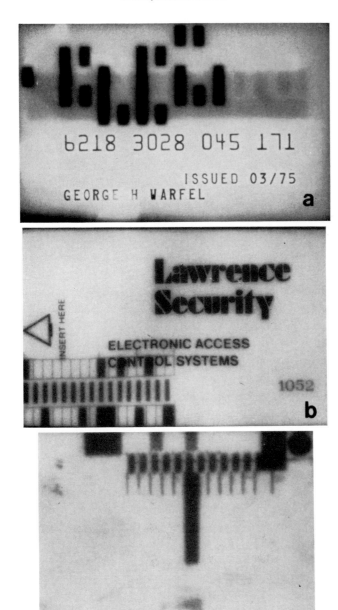

Figure 26. These three ID cards are read by infrared light. Citicard *(a)* is a bank credit card. Cards *(b and c)* are for high-security access control.

missivity. With the black shadows of the Citicard, only one bit per location can be coded. But by using six levels of shade, each location can represent six bits. While this enlarges the coding possibilities, it is unlikely to affect the postencoding schemes that will continue to work only on one-bit code elements. In placing personal ID data into an IR card, the multiple transmissivity offers very little gain.

One of the problems with IR cards is the conflict with other printing. It is the desire of every marketing group to print large, attractive logos on the face of the plastic cards. Unless special inks are used, these graphics mask and interfere with the IR coding. Such masking is often overlooked by the printer as he matches his colors by eye. Great care should be taken in planning graphic emblems over the coded area. While the IR card may seem to lend itself to better aesthetic treatment than the brown magnetic stripes or a field of holes punched over the card, it is not free from restrictions concerning graphics.

The internal coding of IR cards can be done by a printing process similar to that used in printing sequentially numbered tickets. The rotating print wheels in this case are faced with rectangular blocks of code rather than numbers. Also, the wheels are interrelated in a binary fashion, rather than on a decimal (tens) basis. However, printing of code on the core stock prior to lamination can be done automatically; the coding does not have to be done manually.

ULTRAVIOLET ENCODED CARDS

The use of invisible code spots on the card surface was considered by the ABA and rejected. Ironically, it was the ease with which the code could be changed that caused the committee to reject ultraviolet (UV) cards and favor the magnetic stripe.

The advantage of UV coding is that it allows the whole surface of the card to remain available for graphics. In addition, unlike the IR card, the code is over the graphics (yet invisible), and thus there is no restriction on the inks used in printing the logos and instructions. Also, unlike the IR card, the code goes on last, and thus the card can be encoded at the time of issue. This permits machine-readable personal ID data to be included in the UV code.

It would seem that with all these advantages, the UV card would be used widely, but this is not the case. It may come into use as an ID card someday, but it is unlikely.

The principle of operation of the UV card is much like any optically read card. To read the card, it is first inserted into a slot, where it is illuminated by a black light. In response to this light, spots previously printed on the surface of the card glow a brilliant violet. Only the spots glow; the rest of the card is dark. At the time of encoding, the spots were printed in a unique pattern, according to a binary code, and under the UV light, optical sensors can read and decode that pattern. Sensors are cheap solid-state devices, and the light source is usually a filtered fluorescent tube of low wattage.

OPTICAL (VISUAL BAND) ENCODED CARDS

The use of optically encoded cards for ID cards has not met with wide acceptance. These cards, like the UV cards, have a code printed over the face of the card, but in this case, the code is visible. Of course, the card is unattractive, and it is difficult to print any graphics on the card. Because it is easy to alter with any pen or pencil, the card is unsuitable for secure data.

ENCODED HOLES

One of the first plastic cards was a miniature copy of the punched tab card. The encoded holes were punched through, forming the data field. These holes may be read by vacuum, heat, light, or by sensing fingers. These cards are not tamper proof and thus are limited to low-value data cards. In today's market, they compete with the magnetic data cards and with paper-punched cards. In durability, they are superior to both. For personal ID cards, they hardly seem to fill the requirement as well as some other cards.

There is one area where a certain type of punched-hole card is unique; for easy encoding in the field. The cards are made with a full field of holes partially punched. The desired code can then be punched out by a pencil, with the small disks being broken out as needed to create a field of code. Parity bits can be punched along the edge line.

Cards like this can be used for short-term ID cards, but they do not hold up well in everyday use. It is almost impossible to print any detail on the surface, and thus they are unattractive. Their principal use was as an early automatic dialer for a telephone.

EMBOSSED BARS

The card using raised embossed bars in a binary code pattern is not only easily read by a machine sensor, but also leaves an imprint on a carbon paper document that can also be machine read. There are simple and economical machines that make these coded embossments in standard 3/100-inch thick PVC cards, thus permitting easy encodement at the time of issue. These many advantages lead to an early popularity of the bar-coded card. In many cases, the raised bars were a binary representation of embossed digital characters on the same card. This produced a card and an imprinted paper that was both machine and manually readable. It is relatively simple to heat and flatten the bars or dots and equally easy to put new ones in with a hammer and a blunt chisel; thus, the bar code is not considered secure. For a card where fraud is not a problem, the embossed-bar method is a cheap means of entry into a machine-readable paper system. In most new systems, though, more sophisticated methods have replaced the bars.

OPTICALLY READ CHARACTERS

During the days of deliberation, when the ABA was setting standards for the magnetic stripe card, the National Retail Merchants Association (NRMA) made it clear that they would not join in and adopt the magnetic stripe. They felt that it should be possible to manually read whatever data was being machine read. They finally adopted optical character recognition (OCR) as their standard, selecting OCR-A as the font of type for the card. Not only was the machine code manually readable, but it allowed the same machine to read price tags, inventory numbers, and all of the numeric data that is at the retail point of sale.

Just as the ABA standards spurred research in magnetics, the NRMA standard spurred research in optics. Today, there are handheld wands that can read tags, cards, and sheets of paper printed in OCR fonts. These are surprisingly tolerant of operator error in position and speed of the wand. Head angles as far as 8 degrees in either direction can be accommodated, and scan speeds of 3 to 13 inches per second will read properly. Since OCR-A is a font available for typewriters, machine-readable cards could be typed up at the point of issue, containing personal ID data. Although precautions could be taken to prevent card alterations, OCR cards can be easily counterfeited. OCR reading wands are available today from Recognition Products, Inc., in Dallas, Texas.

READING EMBOSSED CHARACTERS

Since the embossed plastic card was introduced in the early 1950s, it has been a favorite ID card. Although the raised characters were designed to imprint on a carbon form-set sales ticket, they are also an easy way to put data on a plastic card, even though the card may never see an imprinter. Embossing machines were designed by many of the business machine manufacturers and are still available today. There are small embossing machines that operate like heavy-strike typewriters, and there are big, computer-controlled "crunchers" that emboss an entire line at one press. With either machine, it is possible to put a name, address, account number, and personal ID data into raised characters.

If the raised characters are in a large, stylized font, they can be read by sensing the height pattern, and for a while, it seemed that machine reading the account number this way might challenge the magnetic stripe. The reading was done by shadows cast from an oblique light source. The method had the advantage that the machine-read data was the same as the human read data, and thus it ensured there was no chance of involving two accounts.

Because there are so many readily available machines for embossing cards, it has occurred to many employers to issue embossed ID cards. It is not a good method if the card is to be considered secure. The characters can be easily flattened and re-embossed with simple handtools. The technique has been widely publicized in the underground press and seems to resurface as a hardy perennial, informing each college graduating class on the skills of altering cards. Embossed characters are primarily for creating imprinted paper forms and are not well suited to ID data.

When embossed characters are to be manually read, it is desirable to coat the raised portion with a color that contrasts with the background. This is called *tipping*. For small operations, it is done manually with a roller, as a printer might ink type for a proof. The bigger presses apply the ink and dry it at a final station in the embossing machine.

PROXIMITY CARDS

A new kind of card solving the problem of having to put a machine-readable card into a slot has been marketed. These cards can be read at a distance of a foot or so from the reader while still in the possession of the owner. This is excellent for access control (low security) where the people going in and out are likely to be encumbered. A file clerk with an armful of paper can have the card on a bracelet, and merely pass by the reader. The reader recognizes the card and unlocks the door. Most likely, the door will have a power opener on it, too. For messengers who have a cart to push, the same system is ideal. For parking lot entrance, the proximity card avoids having to put the card in the slot. The driver merely waves the card at the reader, and the gate goes up.

Of course, there is no personal ID involved in this system. At present it is merely an entry ticket. But identification data could be added. For example, once the card is recognized, a computer system could alert the guard that the cardholder was blonde, female, about twenty-seven-years-old, and of slender build, etc. The guard would only have to compare these features with the person making entry and a fairly secure ID system would be in effect. If the features on record were not known, even to the cardholder, additional protection would be afforded, because an imposter would not know which features to mimic and would thus be forced to make up like a perfect twin. The proximity card, available from Schlage Electronics, Sunnyvale, California, is still new and has possibilities for expansion.

The principle is based on a tiny radio transmitter as a reader. When the field generated by the radio is absorbed by a card, the card's presence is detected. But only cards containing a unique radio circuitry cause this effect. Other proximity cards, tuned to other locations, are not recognized, and certainly ordinary plastic cards do not respond. Most systems recognize any of a group of cards and do not identify particular cards as unique within the group. As solid-state electronics improve, further development in the proximity card can be expected.

Recent developments in miniaturization or large-scale integration (LSI) microcircuits make it possible to put considerable memory and computer power in the plastic card.[12] Such cards have been developed in Europe, are called *Inovatron,* and could be made easily by any North American microprocessor builders. The economics of such a card might seem out of reason at first, but in the next few years, there may be machine-readable computers implanted in the card.

MANUALLY READ CARDS

The majority of cards are read by human beings. In particular, ID cards are almost always read by a human. Even where cards are machine read for transaction or for access control, the identification usually takes place manually. In such cases, the record keeping and the first cut at security is automated, but the actual comparison of reference data with personal data is a visual process. The reference data may be a signature, an encrypted number, a photograph, or physical-description features.

PIN NUMBERS, PASSWORDS, AND CODE WORDS

If a password or personal identification number is associated with a card, the data must not appear on the card in the clear. To put it on in magnetic code or optical (IR) code is not enough, if the card is to be used for ID. Most card-related systems using PIN numbers keep the PIN number on file in the system data bank. This means that all terminals must be on-line, i.e. wired to the central, if the card is to be used at more than one location. Some systems encrypt the number and write it on the magnetic stripe, trusting in the encryption to maintain security. In these systems, the card can be used at any terminal where the decryption logic is installed. While this avoids the expense of having all terminals on-line, it lessens the security of the system.

VISUALLY READ ACCOUNT NUMBERS

Many businesses, wishing to give the appearance of being progressive, forward-looking enterprises, issued cards to their customers. The cards carried account numbers and perhaps some ID data, usually a signature. These cards, however, were often misleading and were only a small step toward automation or security. Even if the cards were embossed with the customer's name and account number, it was not unusual to see the clerk transcribing the number using a ball-point pen. As identification cards, they were usually meaningless.

Some clubs felt that they should look up-to-date and issue what they called ID cards. Usually a new membership number was typed on the card, but it was of no significance. Similar employee cards are seen in small plants. Usually, the cards are only a token effort at controlled access. Certainly, unless they carry some personal data, they are at best only a mild deterrent.

PHOTO IDENTIFICATION CARD

The photo card is the staple of the ID business.[13, 14] Photos are on most driver's licenses and most employee cards. It is required on all passports. Although many people joke about how the pictures do not look like them, the usual photo is hard to cheat. The weak point in the system is at the inspection point. The police and the immigration officers become experts at photo comparison. They seldom see the same person twice in the course of their work, yet they make hundreds of comparisons in a week. The plant guard, however, is in a different situation. He sees the same faces ten or fifteen times a week, yet deals with a total population perhaps as low as a few dozen people. He is also dealing with people in a hurry, and he does not have the authority over the identifyee that police or immigration officers have. Certainly, a plant guard is not going to challenge one of the top executives or one of their secretaries. Thus, the employee badge or card is often not examined as closely as it should be. As long as the potential for close examination exists, the photo is an excellent deterrent to any attempt at false ID, in spite of the fact that it is seldom closely checked.

There are stories about pranksters pasting cartoon pictures over their own and not being challenged. No doubt, there are records of impostors successfully replacing the photos in passports, driver's licenses, and other cards. In many cards, especially the plastic pouch type, it is easy to do. There are cards that use techniques to make such a picture change difficult. The criminal's effort is to steal a card, lift the true photo out and put in a picture of himself, leaving the rest of the card intact.

One deterrent to this is to have the photo taken against a special background that the average imposter would not have available. Thus, the substitute photo would catch the eye. While this seems a simple trick, most employee ID photos today are taken against a white sheet and are easily exchanged. A sophisticated version of this makes the entire card one continuous color photo. This is done with a special camera in which the printed data, unreduced, is photographed onto the same film as the portrait. The portrait, however, is much reduced and is against a special backdrop. The result is a fraud-resistant card. It is produced by R. D. Products, Inc., in Victor, New York. This firm was instrumental in designing the new alien ID cards that contain fingerprints, signatures, and many other ID features, in addition to the photograph.

There are several other ways of preventing photo substitution on picture cards. Most of them have to do with bonding the plastic to the photograph so that it is impossible to remove any part of the data without destroying the card. This may mean chemically transferring the photograph to the plastic stock or binding the photo with an adhesive or embossing a code over part of the photo.

The 3M Corporation of St. Paul has an optical coating that prevents alteration of driver's licenses. This coating reflects an easily detected pattern to columnated light, and any attempt to alter the card upsets this pattern visibly. It is used on California driver's licenses and has sharply reduced alteration and counterfeit.

In an effort to assure adequate comparison by the identifier, a system that examines the card photo via TV is now available. By expanding the card photo to near full size, a much better comparison is possible. This system is described in Chapter 10.

SIGNATURE PANELS

Because of the cost, photos have not been popular on retail credit cards. Since the law requires some method of relating the card-holder to his card, the signature has appeared on almost all retail credit cards.

Because the surface of PVC is glossy and does not take ink, a paperlike signature panel is affixed by a hot-stamp process. Without exception, the panel is too small for a normal signature, usually being $\frac{5}{16} \times 2\frac{3}{4}$ inches. This reduced size makes it difficult to compare the signature on the card with the signature on the sales slip. Also, the rough surface presents a problem. The panel is designed to be exceptionally easy to write on, which makes it an excellent gatherer of dirt. On cards that have been carried and used a great deal, the panel soon dirties so that the signature is hardly readable.

To prevent erasure and replacement of the original signature, these panels have a safety pantagraph background, much like the safety paper on checks. This, too, makes a light pen signature seem to fade into the background and difficult to read.

The most unfortunate part of the signature card, as it is used today, is in the method of issue. Usually, these cards are mailed to the customer, and he is to sign his card upon receipt. This means that a criminal can lift the card from the mails, sign his own name (or that of the cardholder in his own hand), and commence to use the card. Any clerk making a comparison of signatures will find a perfect match. The best way to prevent this is to have the customer come into the bank or store and sign the card after adequate identification procedures. This plan would cause many potential customers to ignore it and some cards would go unused; thus the marketing men tend to oppose such a plan. With the signature panel, as with so many methods of protection, it runs counter to the marketing attitude.

Gasoline credit cards have not relied on the signature as a means of relating the cardholder to the card. They have used the vehicle license as a fraud preventative, with considerable success.

SUMMARY

The plastic "ID card" has become a common item in every purse and wallet in the country. There are many types, but the card with the signature panel and magnetic stripe is standard, with the bank credit cards such as Master Charge and Visa®. The Citicard chose to go its own way with IR coding and has much better control over fraud.

Plant employee cards usually have photos and are manually read at the point of entry.

For parking control, the magnetic spot card is a favorite, with proximity cards gaining because they are easy to use.

It is apparent that no general standard has emerged, either for reading the card or for relating it to its proper holder. The size, shape, and material seem to be generally agreed upon, but technology has yet to produce the other features that are acceptable to all parties.

REFERENCES

1. Barney, W. W.: U. S. Patent No. 3,788,617. Coded Magnetic Card and System for Encoding and Sensing the Same. (Filed June 1972, issued Jan., 1974.)
2. American National Standards Institute: Magnetic stripe encoding for credit cards. ANSI-X 4.16-1973. New York, ANSI, 1973.
3. International Standards Organization: Credit cards-magnetic stripe encoding for trucks one and two 3554, 1st ed. New York, New York, ANSI, 1976.
4. ABA magnetic stripe highly vulnerable to fraud, WSBA staff engineer declares. *American Banker,* Nov. 3, 1972.
5. Linden, L. and Hines, J.: Private interview, July, 1978.
6. Fayling, R. E.: *Fraud Resistant Dual Energy, Dual Layer Magnetic Stripe Credit Cards.* Read before the ABA Bankcard Security Seminar, Louisville, Kentucky, Oct., 1975.
7. Ferdman, M., Lambert, D. W., and Snow, D. W.: *Security Aspects of Bank Card Systems.* MITRE Corp., Washington, D. C., ABA, Sept., 1975.
8. *Identification: Linking People to Plastic.* Internal document, Special Bank Projects, Security Pacific National Bank, Los Angeles, California, Oct., 1974.
9. Svigals, J. and Ziegler, H. A.: Magnetic stripe credit cards: Big business in the offing. *Spectrum, 11(12):* 1974.
10. Nilson, H. S.: Citibank's secret credit card encoding process. *Nilson Report.* Issue no. 95, July, 1974.
11. Swift, D. M.: U. S. Patent No. 4,066,910. Transmissivity Coded Data Card Systems. (Field Apr. 1974, issued Jan., 1978).
12. Reistad, D. L.: Personal communication with the author, May, 1978.
13. Kuhns, R.: Photographic identification. *Security Management, 21(1):* 1977.
14. Logsdon, S. M.: Multi-level security problem solving. *Security World, 14(5):* 1977.

Chapter 9

PASSWORDS, CODES, AND ENCRYPTION

I N CHAPTER 4, it was mentioned that one of the basic methods of identifying a person is by what he *knows*. This does not mean that a person must be of wide knowledge or that the system would measure the knowledge he has and thus identify him. Rather, the system uses some item of knowledge that the identifyee has memorized and an imposter is not likely to know. This item is the password. Also, as a part of the method, this bit of knowledge must be recorded in the system and be available to the part of the system performing the identification. These two factors are fundamental to the password method of ID.

Until the computer became a part of everyday life, password identification for casual transactions was performed primarily by the use of family names. Most banks wrote the depositor's mother's maiden name on the signature card, and this served as the password for phone inquiry or when a new teller was at the window. Some banks asked the patron the amount of his last deposit, and this became a constantly changing password known to both the bank and the depositor. In clubs and lodges, the password was used to identify members. In this case, though, the password was usually the same for all members and thus was not a personal identifier. The military makes extensive use of passwords in radio and telephone communications, to ensure the identity of the parties involved. In corporate funds transfer (often called *wholesale banking*) where large sums of money are transferred between major corporations or banks, passwords are used extensively.[1] These words are kept in books and are constantly changed so that different words appear in each day's messages.

With the coming of shared computer facilities, it became necessary to identify each user as he operated the computer terminal. Not only was this necessary for billing out the time used, but for allowing the user access to his own data bank and his own programs, which were stored at the central facility. The most important purpose of identifying the person at the remote terminal was to assure all other shared-facility users that this party could not access any of their data. Usually one party has no knowledge of the identity of other sharing users. It would not be unusual for two construction contractors to be preparing competitive bids on the same job, each using his own data from his own site survey, and each using his own formulas, but both using the same computer belonging to a computer service company. Only good user identification can assure them that the other has no access to their proprietary files. This user identification is almost always by password.

In all password systems, the basic element is a word (or numbers) known to the parties and not known to the imposter. Of course, the system breaks down if an imposter gains access to the password. It is catastrophic when the impostor acquires the password and it is not known that the password has been compromised. Secrecy is fundamental to the use of the password, and when this secrecy has been breached, the entire system must be notified.

PASSWORD MANAGEMENT

It is secrecy that makes the password method difficult to use. The management of the secret, so it is known to all who need it and absolutely no one else, is a critical task. If the password is used in business, it is desirable that the secret be known by a position or a work station and not a person. This way, the business does not come to a halt when that person is away. Also, if the password can be managed in such a way that the usual person dealing with it cannot take it from the work station, a greater security is achieved. The person cannot give it away, nor can it be taken from him while he is away from his work station.

In the past, in money-transfer systems, this has meant constructing a password from a set of tables or formulas that were too complex to be memorized. The books containing the tables and formulas were kept in vaults. Such protection is time consuming and costly, but has served the banks' money-transfer system for decades. Losses were rare in these systems, and the method served the industry well, even though constructing the passwords was slow. Today, the formula and many of the tables can be put into computers. This not only provides secrecy, but increases accuracy and speed.[2]

With the secret data thus locked up so that a human cannot read it, the protection of the password requires only the protection of the computer. This is entirely possible today, where a whole computer system, a microprocessor, is no larger than a book. One might be more comfortable if the password calculator were the size of a household refrigerator and weighed 1,000 pounds, but by keeping close tab on the input unit, the smaller ones can provide a safety far beyond yesterday's calculators. The important thing is that password calculators should not be shared in any way and should not involve any transmission lines. The microprocessors should be self-contained units, completely visible in their entirety from all sides, and should have only one means of input. Having the secret wrapped up in one readily recognizable piece of hardware means that only theft of the unit must be prevented and good security will be realized. Figure 27 shows one such unit for use in international money transfers by the S.W.I.F.T. system.

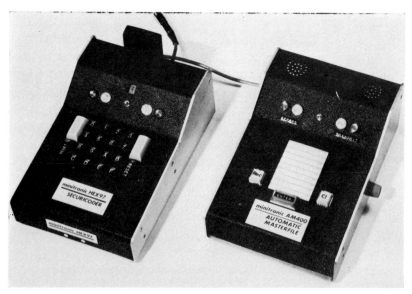

Figure 27. For international funds transfer, identification is computerized by this machine. Most S.W.I.F.T. messages use this method. (Photograph courtesy of Minitronics International, Ltd., London, England.)

Although many money-transfer systems are now using computers to construct passwords, most systems have multiple access from remote points and thus have to contend with the problem of wiretap intrusion on the transmission lines, as well as identifying the user at the remote point. The proponents of such systems point to the advantage that the password encoding and decoding process is in only one location, i.e. the central computer. They also often emphasize that their company has a great excess of big centralized computer power. Future systems, however, will find it better to have the encoding-decoding function in many machines, but with each totally self-contained and with only one keyboard, and that, too, integrated into the same physical unit. If the unit is small enough to be installed in a vault, yet too big to be carried away, a secure system is obtained. This way, there are no transmission lines and only a single hands-on operator for each unit.

The chink in the armor of such a system is in the personnel who build and maintain the system. Someone must know how it works and how to build it.

That person has to supervise the architecture of the system, assuring that no one of the people working for him has access to enough data to compromise the system in the future. Again, reliance can be placed in making the data too complex or too voluminous for it to be memorized. The maintenance on a coding-decoding microprocessor should be zero. It would be unwise to attempt repair on a unit that had been in service; it would be better to destroy it. In fact, the unit should be so constructed that it cannot be accessed for repair (or inspection) without being destroyed. In microcircuitry this does not mean any self-exploding devices, it requires only well-planned packaging. Today's microprocessors are so cheap and so reliable that this is practical.

The catalog of input in a password system must be changed constantly to assure that a chance compromise cannot continue to breach the system. In a computerized password system, this can be done either by sending each location a fresh memory element already loaded or a paper document permitting keyboard entry of the data. In the case of a large, main frame computer, tapes or discs could be sent out. For microprocessors, read-only-memories

(ROM) could be mailed out as chips and plugged in. Keyboard entry would be proper for any type of computer. Secrecy would not be necessary on such inputs, since they would represent such a small part of the coding process. Thus, only routine mail precautions need be observed when distributing these keys.

PIN NUMBERS

The personal identification number is a special case of the password. It is an easy-to-remember number, usually four or five digits that members of the general public use as a secret identity number. Most often, it is used to access automatic teller machines (ATMs),[3] but has also been used for bank transactions at grocery counters.[4] When ATMs and unattended cash dispensers first appeared, the customers were given six-digit numbers to memorize to gain access to the machines. To use the machine, the customer first put his card in the slot. The card would be machine read, thus identifying the account to be accessed. The customer would then enter his PIN number into a keyboard, and if it matched the one on file for that card or account number, the transaction was permitted. In the event of errors, a second or third try was usually allowed. In later models, the customer could choose his own PIN number, making it much easier to remember.

In selecting the PIN method, the attempt was to reduce the human being to the level of the machine by making the human memorize digits and activate push buttons. Of course, this was only natural, since the machine was unattended and usually not an intelligent machine. There are now thousands of these machines installed in bank driveways or in airports and available at all hours with no one around to maintain security (Fig. 28).

When a PIN is used in an unattended system as above, the reference number may be recorded either in the machine or in a central computer bank or on the patron's card. Each method has an exposure to compromise. Some banks limit the patron to one machine, usually the machine where his account is kept or perhaps one machine of his selection. This, of course, is the one near his work or home. To permit the customer to use more machines, all ATMs in a system are frequently interconnected to a central file by telephone lines. In such a network, there is the risk of in-

Figure 28. Automatic teller machine for dispensing cash after banking hours. Customer is identified by PIN number and card. (Photograph courtesy of Docutel Corporation, Dallas, Texas.)

trusion by wiretap. Yet, if this is to be avoided by putting all active PIN numbers in all machines, the management of the secret file becomes difficult. In large systems, there is a constant turnover of numbers as accounts are opened and closed. There is also the possibility of compromise of PIN lists by maintenance personnel. Not only do bank employees have to visit the machine to replenish cash (and remove cash, if it takes deposits), but ATMs are sophisticated electromechanical machines, and technicians must effect constant maintenance and repairs. These technicians are usually not bank employees and often not even employees of the machine vendor. Thus, allowing them access to a machine with a PIN list in it involves a certain risk. To put the PIN on the card, thus avoiding on-premises file storage, means it must be encrypted, which itself involves risk and cost. No matter how it is treated, the PIN, because it is nothing but a secret group of digits, represents risk.

The PIN number has its supporters, many of them heavily biased because they have invested in machines and systems that use it. ATMs at fifty thousand dollars each (installed) represent a large investment. Considerable support also comes from those who cannot find anything else to replace it. Certainly, the PIN number served to introduce the ATM and is still the only reasonable way to provide customer identification with unattended machines.

From a critical viewpoint, PIN evolved because it was a cheap, unsophisticated way to make a machine accept secret data. The customer was pushed into an uncomfortable, but tolerable, position and made to fit the system by memorizing a unique number. Only later came systems allowing customers a choice of numbers. Before this option became available, 70 percent of the customers wrote the PIN number someplace near their ATM card[5]–if not on the card itself! Also popular, and still in use, is the contract in which the bank and the customer agree that the bank assumes minimal responsibility for funds dispensed to the wrong party. The customers accept this, but it seems unfair.

Basic to all of the problems is that the password, or PIN, is not a natural thing. It is imposed on the customer by the machine. Not being natural, it can exist anywhere–written, memorized, on magnetic memory, encrypted, or in the clear. It can also be transferred, often unwittingly. Unlike a card or a key, when transferred, it actually multiplies and is not missing from its original place. A half-dozen people can know a PIN, and each of them may think he is the only one. A thief can steal a PIN, perhaps by observation, and the true holder never knows that his secret is gone. This is not true of an artifact such as a card or a key. If someone steals your keys, you miss them soon, perhaps in time to prevent the theft of your car or at least get the lock changed on your home. But the PIN thief has ample time to sell your number to a card broker, who will then send one of his men to "borrow" and duplicate your ATM card. Also, the PIN, if it is to be kept secret, must be under the complete control of issuer and the user. This means that there would have to be a different PIN number for every card in the user's wallet. Such a proliferation of numbers would only lead the customer to write down his list of PINs, thus losing the security. Shared PIN numbers are not feasible where different cards carry widely different cash limits, and thus different risk and security boundaries.

In some ID systems where there is an attendant, the patron or identifyee enters a memorized number into a keyboard, and then the attendant or identifier enters another number into his keyboard, and a resultant number appears in a display.[6] For such systems, the secret number is only in the mind of the identifyee, but the other two numbers are printed on the card or the passbook carried by the customer. Of course, the mathematical manipulation of the two entered numbers is also a secret, and it is locked into the electronics beneath the keyboard. As long as the memorized number remains a secret, the system is secure. If the patron forgets his number or feels it may have been learned by someone else, a new number can be selected. In this case, the clerk's number remains the same, and the new resultant number is typed onto the card as soon as it is obtained. The resultant number is generated by simply going through the same procedure with the patron entering whatever new number he has selected. Nowhere is the secret number recorded, unless the patron makes that error himself. The card in this system has only the two numbers on it, in addition to any data or artistic work the card issuer wishes to use. It is not possible to preprint these cards, because the resultant number is dependent on the patron's choice of secret number. However, it is simple enough to write this number on a panel provided, once it is known. Since there is no reason for these numbers to become involved in a processing system, they are not usually embossed. Often the card is only heavy paper. It is wise to encase these in a plastic case to give them durability and to prevent the patron from writing anything (especially his PIN) on the card.

This method is manufactured as Identikey® by Atalla Technovations, Inc., of Sunnyvale, California, in either stand-alone units or as part of a network system (Fig. 29). Even in the network, though, the PIN is never recorded. The system is available with

Figure 29. The Atalla Technovations' Identikey provides top-security PIN number or password identification. (Photograph courtesy of Atalla Technovations, Inc., Sunnyvale, California.)

alpha-numeric ten-key entry devices, similar to the familiar telephone Touch-Tone® dialing system. By using three alpha characters on each digital key, the patron may choose a word or a name, rather than a number, for his secret password. Although he memorizes an alphabetical word, the keyboard reads it as a group of digital characters. This approach also eliminates the most common error in the entry of memorized number groups, i.e. transposition.

TRANSMISSION AND RECORDING OF PASSWORDS

In all systems, the password or PIN must be concealed in some fashion, wherever it exists. If the patron insists on writing it down, some effort should be made at concealment, such as making it look like a phone number, or raising each digit by five. Within the electronic system, a fairly sophisticated method of encryption must be employed, since hundreds or thousands of numbers exist, along with their account numbers and the account holders' names.

In a network system, the encryption must not only protect the identity of the user and his password, but must conceal the transaction message itself. If the PIN were being used for ID as an entry or access control, encryption would also be required before transmission of the numbers to a central security file for matching.

In a transaction system, where an instruction message accompanies the account number and the PIN, encryption is not only for secrecy, but also for accuracy. The instruction message may involve the transfer of a specified amount to a certain account. It is essential that the account number and the amount be absolutely correct. The accuracy encryption serves a different purpose than the secrecy encryption, but is equally important.[7] The accuracy is also subject to attack, since there are unscrupulous people who would alter the amount transferred in their own favor or change the payee account number to their own or that of an accomplice.

ENCRYPTION, CODES, AND CIPHERS

The technology of cryptography has occupied some of the greatest minds in history. Even today, there are many amateur cryptologists who enjoy it as a mental exercise.

Basically, one encrypts information in an attempt to conceal it from all but the intended user. The data may be in a code, or in a cipher, but in either case, the intent is to make it secret.

A code is typically a substitution method in which there is no regard for maintaining similar size of the data. For example, the letter *P* may be substituted for the phrase "Pay to the order of" in a code, or the word *zebra* may be substituted for the letter *Z*. Because of its nature, a code often has no logic to its structure, perhaps not even as much as the above examples where the letters and the first character of the corresponding phrases are the same. If a code were used to generate a personal identification password, using account number and name,[8] there would be some possibility of compromise, because the account number and the person's name are so readily obtained from a check. Checks circulate so widely that a criminal could conceivably photocopy thousands of checks as they passed through the commercial system external to bank processing. With sufficient volume of data and a computer at his disposal, a code could be broken. As mentioned before, he could then use the coded passwords freely, since they were known to him, but not missing from their usual place–the user's mind. If coded passwords are used, it is essential that they have no connection with the account number or the account holder's name. It is best that the account holder have free choice of the original password.

A cipher is a different approach to concealing a password or a message. A *cipher* is a mathematical manipulation that results in a character for character substitution. For example, the character *A* may be replaced by the character *B*, and *B* by *C*, etc., making the message appear to be garbage. Yet, it is easily deciphered by anyone who knows the trick. The translation of a cipher follows a set of mathematical rules, called a *key*.

As with codes, because the input data, the name, and account or employee number are so easily obtained, a simple or even a relatively complex cipher is subject to compromise when it is used to generate a password based on related data. Ciphers, like codes, have their best application when the text of the information is not easily guessed by the person breaking the message. Military messages are often padded with meaningless phrases to make the encryption more secure. If a password is enciphered, it should be some random word that could not be guessed by anyone attempting to break the cipher.

With codes, and even more so with ciphers, the method of encrypting (and, of course, the corresponding decryption) can become complex. With the aid of the computer, sophistication previously never thought possible is easily attained. Either method is perfectly suited to computer computation. Regrettably, the computer is also available to the criminal who attempts to break the encryption. Codes formerly thought invincible can now be readily broken with a few hours' time on a computer. It was easy when a code could be constructed in a few minutes and would take weeks of mathematical manipulation to break. One only had to change codes every four days to keep ahead of the criminal. Now, even if it takes thousands of times longer to break than to make a code, that may be comparing ten minutes with one millisecond, and good security requires a code change every two minutes. However, such a frequent change is not impossible with adequate key management.

KEY MANAGEMENT

In any cryptographic system, the control of the key is vital. If the key falls into the hands of a criminal, he does not have to waste time breaking the method. He is home free. To maintain good security, the key distribution must be limited and controlled. The loss of a key, even temporarily, must be reported to all key holders, and new, totally independent keys must be distributed. Within one organization, or on one premises, as in access control by PIN number, this would not present a problem. But for nationwide use by thousands of competitive organizations, it can be difficult. In the latter case, it is almost essential to go to the self-contained microprocessor, which is small enough to visually supervise but too large to steal.

REVERSIBLE AND IRREVERSIBLE CIPHERS

In the technology of cryptography, there are two basic kinds of cipher: the reversible and the irreversible. As the terms imply, a reversible method permits a concealed word to be decrypted back to its clear equivalent if the key is known. The irreversible one does not allow such a simple method. In all rational ID systems, the task is really one of verification, i.e. answering the question "Is this person who he purports to be?" Thus, either reversible or irreversible methods can be used. For messages of text, there are advantages to each that do not exist in the other, thus, the method used depends on the circumstances surrounding the message, the system, and the business involved.

Because of the ease of encryption and decryption by computer, many unique uses have been proposed for this skill. Of course, concealing a personal ID password is one use. Another is for maintaining secrecy for privacy in transactions. Often, large transfers of money signal a corporate shift or a marketing move that should be proprietary knowledge. To keep these big-money transfers secret, encryption of the transfer message is advised. Frequently, coding is used to gain brevity in message format, especially where messages are repeated periodically. Codes are also used to assure accuracy. By adding code words constructed from the text of the message, the recipient can verify that the text has been correctly transmitted by comparing these "check words" in the message. In some systems, the accuracy and the secrecy codes are combined into one utility code. Although encryption has not played an important role in personal ID at the employee entrance gate, it has long been employed in telegraphic funds transfer and is destined to be an essential part of the electronic funds transfer services. It is now and will remain vital to distributed or time-shared computer systems.

PASSWORDS IN SHARED COMPUTER NETS

The use of passwords in shared computer networks has not given the concern that it has in banking circles. This is primarily because the shared net is operated by professionals and not by the general public. This makes for fewer users per entry point and allows physical control over the entry point. Also, with a limited number of users per terminal, a tighter password management program can be maintained. In these systems, passwords can be alphabetic, because the keyboards are usually typewriter type, and passwords can be longer and even of record at the input point, since the public is not using the machine. Another distinct advantage of the remote terminal is that at each terminal the group of users are all known to each other. It is unlikely that one would cheat on the system knowing that the others might see him. Even though he were cheating someone outside the group and not cheating them, he would be exposed as a cheater. Of course, it is possible that the entire group in corporation A might steal a password and access the data of corporation B, but the odds are small. There is likely to be an honest man somewhere in the group or one who thought he was left out.

It is unlikely that the password will be replaced in shared-computer network facilities for some time to come.[9]

NATIONAL BUREAU OF STANDARDS ALGORITHM

At the center of a heated controversy is the encryption circuit favored by the National Bureau of Standards (NBS). This has been proposed for enciphering message text, as well as passwords.

The system, first devised by IBM, is termed a *block cipher*. It operates on sixty-four bits of data in a block, with a sixty-four-bit block encryption key.[10] There are fifty-six meaningful bits and eight bits of parity check. The basic algorithm does not need be kept secret, as long as the key is known only to the sender and receiver.

The algorithm, a hard computer program, first processes the data through an initial permutation, equalizing the sixty-four-bit input block into two halves. Then, each half is modified by the encryption key separately, recirculating through the manipulation sixteen times. Finally, another (inverse) permutation combines the halves, and a new and encrypted sixty-four-bit output block results.[11] It is not an easy process to grasp and would be unthinkable, except as a computer process, but as long as keys are kept secret, it is a safe method. The NBS estimates it would take hundreds of years to break the code.[12] The algorithm consists of nearly 16,000 electronic gates, which, with today's technology, can be put onto one large-scale, integrated chip. The chip can be packaged in a 2-inch-square plastic block and sold for around thirty dollars.

Recently, the proposal to use the chip with several keys has come under attack.[13] Martin Hellman of Stanford University does not agree with the NBS that years would be required to break the key. His estimate is half a day, and he argues for expanded keys.[14] Congress, however, has declared the NBS algorithm as "more than adequate for at least a five to ten year time span for the unclassified data for which it is used."[15] While this gives the encryption module official sanction, the word *unclassified* tends to raise questions. Presumably, the term refers to military classifications. The NBS standard also received strong support at a meeting called specifically to discuss the method.[10]

A REVOLUTION IN CRYPTOGRAPHY?

From M.I.T. (Massachusetts), Stanford (California), and Hebrew University (Jerusalem) have come proposals for one-way cryptographic systems.[16] Similar to the irreversible method, these depend on "trapdoor one-way functions," well known in encryption. The method is a proposal to solve message security for everyday business messages. With it, the sealed first-class envelope would be obsolete, and electronic messages would be used.

The plan is to have each company that expects incoming messages to publish its own key for cryptographic messages. These keys would be on file in each major center of business, just as phonebooks are. Anyone wishing to send a message would use the public key of the destination party. Only the destination party has the decode key, and thus only they can interpret the message.

Obviously, this system relies on the fact that knowing the encode key does not allow the message to be decoded.

The proponents of this technique claim that electronic funds transfer can take place with complete secrecy by using this method. To identify the sender, the commitment part of the message would be coded so that the recipient could only decode it by using the public code of the sender, which was on file in his city. Thus, even the origin of the message could be kept secret, and the recipient would be sure that the message was genuine and not sent by an impostor.

The idea is not farfetched, and the codes could be on file as computer chips and called on by dialing up a central file and sending messages through them. Paper would exist only at the original and destination machines. The transmission from keyboard to near central would be in the sender's local code. The rest of the distance would be traveled in the receiver's public code, which only he could break. The commitment signature would be in a combination and would have to be returned to the receiver's local center for decoding, thus authenticating the message.

All of this would incur no more than a few seconds' delay in the total message. It may come sooner than expected.

NEW VERSION OF PIN

One of the flaws in the PIN number is that it is so readily transferred.

The PIN can be given, along with the card, to an employee or agent and used to perform a transaction in which the party represents the cardholder. And, while the card can be retrieved, the PIN is forever in the mind of another.

The PIN can also be written down and thus stolen and used by another person. It can also be taken by duress—the holder would no doubt blurt out the four-digit PIN to a man with a gun. Then, the gunman, having obtained his victim's wallet, would withdraw funds from the account.

To prevent this transfer by accident or through duress, and yet preserve the benefits of the PIN number, I.D. Code of Palm Springs, California, has devised a new approach to the memorized password. The system uses the fundamental "what the party *recognizes*," as mentioned in Chapter 4. The hardware is a display panel (Fig. 30) on which a number of stylized representations or symbols are permanently inscribed. This display is identical wherever the method is used. Under each symbol, there is a numeric display of one character, which is constantly changed.

To enroll as a user of this password system of ID, the customer selects three or four symbols that strike his fancy. For example, a rancher might select the gun, the hat (the Western), and the horse, as shown in Figure 30. Each time he is called upon to identify himself, he does so by using the digits under these symbols as his temporary PIN number. The next time, these numbers are different, but the central computer knows what numbers were displayed and which three symbols represent this particular customer. Thus, identification is accomplished. Under duress, the identifyee would be hard pressed to describe his chosen symbols. Even if he said "gun, hat, and horse" the display might contain two or three hats and a rifle as well as a pistol. The would-be impostor has a small chance in this system. It is also possible to use meaningless sym-

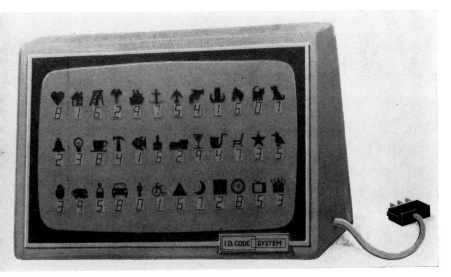

Figure 30. By recognizing a pattern of familiar symbols, a PIN number is generated. The numbers under the symbols are randomly generated and are never the same twice. (Photograph courtesy of I.D. Code, Inc., Palm Springs, California.)

bols that are easy to recognize and remember but difficult to describe–thus defeating the criminal who tries to take the memorized symbols by threat. This system bases its success on the fact that the symbols are easier to remember and harder to give away than a number. It is a PIN number, with the disadvantages removed.

CHANGE IS COMING

Up to now, secrecy in business has depended largely on the sealed first-class message envelope or on private courier, except in the area of corporate funds transfer. Now, with the demand for speedy transactions and immediate identification of the participants, the computer can change all of this. With good crytography and good computer engineering, doing business in a paperless fashion will soon be prevalent.

REFERENCES

1. Cable authenticated faster, cheaper. *Banking, 67(8):* 1975.
2. Hall, Robert A.: EFT in wholesale banking: Computers begin talking to computers. *Banking, 70(5):* 1978.
3. Zimmer, L. F.: *Cash Dispensers and Automated Tellers.* Park Ridge, New Jersey, *Payment Services Correspondents,* 1977.
4. First Federal of Lincoln begins POS funds transfer service. *Payment Systems Newsletter, 6(1):* 1944.
5. Ernst, C. L., (Ed.): *An Assessment of Less Cash/Less Check Technology.* NSF First Phase Report. Washington, D. C., Arthur D. Little, Apr., 1974.
6. PIN systems emerge as a better ID. *Savings and Loan News, 99(6):* 1978.
7. Osterberg, R.: *Security, Privacy and Accuracy in EFT Networks.* Chicago, U. S. League of Savings Associations, Apr., 1976.
8. Clark, C. B., Huffman, D. A., and Zeidler, H. M.: *Security Requirements for Unattended Teller Machines.* New York, MINTS, July, 1973.
9. Wood, H. M.: *The Use of Passwords for Controlled Access to Computer Resources.* Washington, D. C., NBS, May, 1977.
10. Branstad, D. K. (Ed.): *Computer Security and the Data Encryption Standard.* NBS Special Publication no. 500-27. Washington, D. C., NBS, Feb., 1978.
11. Jeffry, S. and Branstad, D.: Data encryption. *Electro '77,* Paper No. 30-4, New York, New York, IEEE.
12. NBS backs data encryption circuit. *Computer Decisions.* Rochelle Park, N. J., Hayden Publishing Co., May, 1975.

13. NBS algorithm hoax: Real or imaginary? *Nilson Report.* Issue no. 179, Jan., 1978.
14. Bain, G.: How to keep your records secret. *Bank Systems and Equipment, 15(4):* 1978.
15. Senate Select Committee on Intelligence: Washington, D. C., U. S. Congress, Apr., 1978.
16. Cryptography: On the brink of revolution? *Science, 117:* 1977.

Chapter 10

IDENTIFICATION BY FACIAL FEATURES

A S IN ALL TYPES OF IDENTIFICATION, ID by facial features is a matter of comparing a questioned or unknown element with a known reference element. In this case it is a questioned face with a known face. As in fingerprints and signatures, the comparison is a form comparison, but the face is a much more complex form. A signature can be adequately compared in black and white and so can a fingerprint. In Chapter 5, it was pointed out that the new video fingerprint systems enhance the prints by reducing any grey shades to either black or white, thus facilitating form comparison. A face, though, is best compared if both the questioned and the reference are not only in shades but in color. The face, unlike fingerprints and signature, is usually compared out of scale by as much as 10 : 1. This is because of the problem of filing life-size photos.

Most people readily admit that they know nothing of fingerprint comparison and leave it to the experts. There are no amateurs in the field of fingerprint identification. In handwriting analysis, however, there are both professionals and a large body of amateurs. There are also thousands of untrained clerks who make an effort at signature comparison when a customer cashes a check or signs a credit slip. But in the area of face recognition, there are no professionals, and all people consider themselves equally competent. Every court has seen its fingerprint experts and handwriting analysists. But one never hears of a face-recognition expert.

The strange lack of professionals has left the skill without a working vocabulary and without texts or references. There is no standard approach to the recognition of faces. Where fingerprints have their terms (whorls, tented arches, and bifurcations, etc.), which are well defined to the professional and unknown to most laymen, the verbal description of a face involves such long phrases as, "the distance between the eyes," "the fullness of the lips," or "the roundness of the cheeks." In every other skill or craft, two

168

practitioners of the same background use professional terms that permit them to convey entire paragraphs in one word. To describe a face, however lengthy sentences must be used because there are no words available.

The lack of standardized terminology has been noted in police work, and some words are beginning to develop. However, police most often try to get a description of a face from someone outside of their profession who is not practiced at verbalizing or at recognition. The police rely on likeness comparisons by producing standard photographs and asking the person to point out similarities between the photo and the person they are trying to describe. This not only eliminates the description-in-words procedure but triggers the thinking and hastens the decision making process. By using these photos, the description becomes a series of Yes or No answers. In computer language, one would say that the analog process had been reduced to a sequence of one-bit decisions.

In addition to being difficult to describe, the face is not static like a fingerprint or a completed signature. The "expression" is always changing. When a face is captured in a photo for a reference item in the identification procedure, the same facial attitude in the subject must be created when comparison must be made. The attitude or expression, however, is the result of emotion, fatigue, surroundings, and a host of other influences. The identifier must try to put the identifyee in the same attitude as when the photo was taken, to facilitate the comparison. This is not always possible, making facial comparison a difficult means of ID.

FACES ARE A WHOLE

Most people are unable to break down their recognition process where faces are involved. Unless the subject has an outstanding feature, such as a scar or a birthmark, the face is usually recognized as a whole. Some researchers who have studied the facial-recognition process have thought this surprising, yet it is rather typical of all visual recognition. The gasoline service-station attendant sees the whole car and identifies it as a certain model, make, and even names the year of manufacture. But, he can not describe the shape of the grille. The international symbol for the handicapped may be seen many times, but who can recall which way the wheel chair is going? This holistic viewing of an entire scene is typical,[1] and while it helps in recognizing friends, it makes it difficult to describe them so that someone else might identify them in our absence.

An effort at description of a face is often helped by feedback. Visual feedback is used by police artists in trying to get a description from a witness. The artist sketches what the person says and then asks if it is correct. Frequently, the describer is able to improve on his statement by pointing out errors or omissions in the sketch. The artist can also improve his sketch by questioning and, as mentioned previously, by showing photos of people and pointing to features in question.

PHOTO IDENTIFICATION CARD

The plastic ID card or badge, with a small color photo on it, has become the standard in employee identification.[2] It is also the most used ID on driver's licenses. This is popular because everybody is considered expert in recognizing faces and does it instantly. Thus, the photo ID requires no training of the identifier. The method also requires no equipment in the system once the card is made. What is overlooked is that an unaided and untrained "expert" is often wrong and easily duped. Every city has a card shop where counterfeit cards, badges, and driver's licenses of all types can be bought. Some of them are remarkably good copies. It is also easy to alter most photo ID cards by changing the photo. Thus, the criminal needs only a photograph and a stolen card. Unless there is some way of excluding cards that have been reported lost, the impostor has no problem at the entry gate.

There are several ways of preventing card alteration. The simplest is to bond the photograph and all other graphic data into the plastic and bond all lamination layers together. This method, as opposed to sealing the card in a plastic envelope, means the card will appear mutilated if an attempt is made to alter any part of it.[3] Most good-quality card and badge manufacturers offer a line of plastics that are so bonded, as well as cheaper cards. The disadvantage of such systems is that they do not lend themselves to being done at the plant location. The plastic envelope type can be made in a few minutes in the personnel offices by using instant-developing photos. Cameras and card-sealing machines are available from many companies, including Laminex, Inc., Matthews, North Carolina; General Binding Corporation, Northbrook, Illinois; and Instant Identification Systems Corporation, Falls Church, Virginia. Most of these firms also offer a line of photo ID cards made in their own plant from negatives and card information mailed in to them.

A unique and secure card that can be made at the location is an engraved photo card. A standard passport photo is used as a copy source. The engraving unit actually cuts through the dark top layer of the plastic card, exposing the white inner material, making a duplicate of the photo, much like a halftone. The engraving head is mechanically driven to etch the image as a scanner moves over the passport photo, electrically commanding the engraver to make varying sizes of cut to represent corresponding shades of grey of the photo. The machine is a German product available in this country through HCM Corporation, Great Neck, New York. A similar product is available from Fuji Electric Company of Japan.

As an aid to the plant guard, closed-loop TV systems that scan the photo on the card and take a full-face shot of the employee as he stands in a booth are available. The two images can be put side by side on a split screen, with a knob to control the scale. By having the pictures close and of the same size, comparison is easy. Such a system also permits the guard to monitor many locations from one guard center. A video record can be maintained for future recall by taping the live image. The TV live shot could also be frozen by video replay techniques, thus providing a static image for the guard to compare with the static reference photo. The booth can also be equipped with a metal detector and a sniffer that detects explosives if the plant security requires that level of safety. To prevent substitution of pictures in such a system, the photos can be first taken through a scrambling lens and then descrambled in the TV camera optical system.[4]

The scrambled photo has the disadvantage that it provides no ID after the employee has entered the plant. Much of the protection in employee badge systems occurs because the employee wears his badge in the open during the shift, and anyone has the opportunity of noticing a mismatch or an altered badge. With the scrambled photo card this would not be possible, unless two photos were used, one a plain photograph and the other scrambled. Scrambling lenses can be made so complex that the two photos side by side would not provide a clue for making a counterfeiting lens. Alternatively, the pictures could be different views and thus make it impossible to break the scrambling formula.

The scrambling method is in the experimental phase at Opticode of New Orleans and could be adapted to any of the TV card systems, such as Mardix, Inc., Mountain View, California, or Vicon Industries, Plainview, New York. Another way to avoid picture substitution in the TV method is to have the photo on video file and not on the card. The employee then enters his employee number into a keyboard (or inserts a machine-readable card), and the picture appears on the TV screen in the guardhouse beside the employee's own live image. If at least three digits of his number are further treated as a secret PIN number, an extremely secure multimodal system results.

With or without TV-aided visual comparison, there is the option of a color photo or black and white. The cost of color photos compared to black and white is not a big factor, but if the card is to be transmitted over a TV link, there can be a considerable difference in cost. Many plant security people think that black-and-white photos make better reference pictures, because the comparison can be made on features only. This is especially true when the subject has dyed hair or a deep tan since the photo was taken.

MULTIMODAL PICTURE CARD SYSTEM

Although not yet offered by any vendor, an extremely secure identification system can be envisioned in which the card carries two photos, one scrambled and the other plain, and a machine-readable number. Upon entering the clearance booth, the employee inserts the card into a slot and the number is read, calling up a video file full-face picture on the upper left of the TV monitor in the guard office. A live mug shot of the employee is shown on the lower left of the screen, and on the right side of the screen are images of the two pictures scanned from the card, one properly unscrambled. If the guard is satisfied with the comparison, he requests the employee to enter a PIN number in the keyboard beside the card slot. This is compared automatically, so that the guard has no knowledge of the number. If that match is satisfactory, the door opens, admitting the employee. Such a system proves–

1. that the identifyee has a card (system rejects any card reported lost or stolen);
2. that the identifyee looks like the photos on the card;
3. that the scrambled photo was originally taken with the mate to the descrambling lens;
4. that the proper memorized secret number was known by the identifyee.

It would still be possible to defraud the system, especially with collusion from the true card owner, but it would take considerable effort. The system could suffer breakdown in any one phase and still be reasonably secure. If the video file were inoperative, the scrambled photo would still provide a reference picture. If the card-scanning TV camera were broken, the card number plus video file would be a backup. Even if the live-face camera were not functioning, the system would assure a relationship between the bearer and the card (the PIN number) and the card and the video file. The plain picture would serve as ID throughout the shift. As an added protection, the photo portion of the card could be kept in a rack at the gate like a time card. This way, the would-be imposter would be hard pressed to make up to look like the picture. He would have to make up to look like his victim as seen live, or work from some other photo. If the scrambled photo were a profile shot, another degree of protection could be added by giving the guard the option to choose a profile camera for the live image. Profiles are extremely hard to alter. Theatrical putty is deceptive at a distance but easily detected at close range because of its lack of pores and blemishes.

COMPUTER RECOGNITION OF FACES

The lack of standard procedures and terminology hampered the early approaches to computer recognition of faces. Traditionally, the first approach to a computer selection has been to computerize the human approach. To computerize a manual bookkeeping system is easy because people now doing the job can be asked to provide a step-by-step analysis of what they do. But to computerize the recognition of faces, much time had to be spent learning how it was being done by humans.

The leader of the small group of researchers in this field is Professor Leon P. Harmon of Case Western Reserve University, Cleveland, Ohio. In an effort to find how people perform identification from facial features, he had a group of people examine twenty-two photos and list the most outstanding features in order of importance.[5] The twenty-two subjects were selected to have no glaring idiosyncrasies, and thus the group was working with normal faces. Such features as tiny ears or thick lips were noted by the group. From these tabulated remarks, a standard list of thirty-five features was compiled. Using this list as a scorecard, a group of ten trained observers examined 256 photographs and rated each feature on a scale of one to five. Of course such ratings are completely relative, but are relative to all of the faces the rater had observed in his life, not necessarily relative within the 256 faces he was rating. It was found that only twenty-one of the features were important, and these were retained as a standard list for future experiments (Table V).

Using these twenty-one features, each rated from one to five over a field of 256 subjects, the numerical data was put into a computer for analysis. The computer was able to describe mathematically an average of these faces. It was further able to name the one face that was closest to this average. It could select the two most similar or the ten most similar pairs and the two least similar by merely manipulating the numerical data.

In this test, the computer did the analysis, once it was informed of the characteristics. Admittedly, the pattern-recognition art has not yet reached a stage where the computer can gather its own data, but the day is near.

If recognition could be done from face profile only, the computer could be made to gather its own data. By taking a TV camera shot of a profile under bright light with a background of a known pattern and color, the video image of the face profile

TABLE V

TWENTY-ONE SELECTED FACIAL FEATURES FOR
IDENTIFICATION*

Hair	*Mouth*
Coverage	Lip Thickness
Length	(Upper)
Texture	(Lower)
Shade	Lip overlap
Forehead	Width
Eyebrows	*Cheeks*
Weight	*Eyes*
Separation	Opening
Ears	Separation
	Shade
Length	*Nose*
Protrusion	
Chin	Length
	Tip
	Profile

* From L. D. Harmon, The Recognition of Faces, *Scientific American, 229(5):*
1973. Courtesy of *The Scientific American,* New York, New York.

could be extracted. This profile curve, the boundary between the
known background pattern and the lack of it, could then be
digitized and entered into a computer for analysis. The scan takes
less than one second.

Once digitized, various significant points could be selected by
the computer and distance values assigned, again by the computer.
Professor Harmon, under an Air Force contract, has studied profiles, using statistical methods on a PDP-11/45 computer.[6] The
chosen features are shown in Figure 31. These points were chosen
because they can be clearly defined from a profile trace, not because they were known to be unique or clearly identifying. Tests
were then run to see if these points could be used to identify people.
This is the reverse of the full-face study of 1973, where features
were selected because they were known to be unique identifying
characteristics. The approach was taken because it was best suited
to the computer. It is not the usual situation to use only the profile
in identifying a person by their face. Thus, it was necessary to start
from scratch and pick features that might serve and then test to
see if they would.

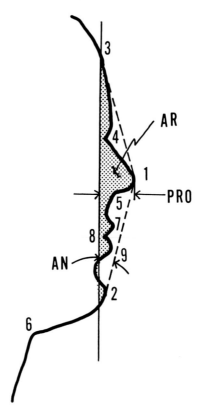

Figure 31. The profile, though seldom used in manual recognition, is the best suited to machine analysis. (From L. D. Harmon and W. F. Hunt, Automatic Recognition of Human Face Profiles, *Computer Graphics and Image Processing*, 1977. Courtesy of Academic Press, New York.)

To give value to the selected feature points, distances between them were calculated. (*Note:* Because there is no easy mark representing the top limit of a profile curve, point 3 was established so that the 1 to 3 distance equaled 1 to 2.) Additional data was supplied from drawing a straight line from points 2 to 3. Using this line as a boundary, the total area between the two was calculated and logged as *AR*. The angle between this line and line 1 to 2 (angle 3-2-1) was entered as *AN*. The distance between this line and point 1 was calculated as *PRO*. Two last elements were taken to represent the bumpiness or kinkiness of the profile curve. Either extremely thin and wrinkled skin or fat and bubbly skin tend to show this trait. The computer was programmed to calculate the radius of curvature and the sharpness with which the curve changes direction, of many points between 1 and 3 and also 1 and 2. These were manipulated into an average and labeled *WU* and *WD* for wiggle-up and wiggle-down.

In the test, many other angles and distances were used and cast out. Finally, nine measurements were accepted as meaningful (Table VI). Using these nine, a profile can be classified and filed, and the file can be searched without human assistance. Since the data is digital, it can be transmitted over standard cross-country data circuits or can be called out verbally over a telephone where no computer is available. A profile curve could even be made by a shadow technique or from a photo, and all but *AR, WU,* and *WD* could be measured by simple draftsman tools. Perhaps some means could be devised so that these could be approximated. Certainly, the curve could be transmitted by facsimile faster than a signature or a fingerprint. Unless a subject were mutilated by accident or crime, the profile could be obtained from someone unconscious or dead, since the normal facial attitude is used. Expression, which so strongly affects a full-face picture, has a slight effect on profile.

The method has some disadvantages. Probably the most difficult one is that it is not a computerized version of a human skill. We seldom see another person in profile, and seldom with the face at rest. This makes it difficult to grasp the method, and the inclination is to reject it. The full-face method described before is much more understandable and also lends itself to successful interac-

TABLE VI

NINE COMPUTER-RECOGNIZED FEATURES OF A PROFILE*

1. Nose tip	6. Throat
2. Chin	7. Upper lip
3. Forehead	8. Mouth
4. Bridge	9. Lower lip
5. Nose bottom	

* From L. D. Harmon, S. C. Kuo, P. F. Ramig, and J. Raudkivi, *Identification of Human Face Profiles by Computer.* First-year report to Air Force, 1976. (Under contract AF-30602-75-C-0121.) Courtesy of L. D. Harmon.

tion between the computer file and human beings. If it were necessary to enter the file with only a witness's description of the subject's face, the profile search would undoubtedly fail for lack of accurate input data. The full-face file could produce a list of likely subjects, especially if the entry data were taken by a skilled police artist.

In the profile test, as in the full-face test, the work was done from photographs, to maintain control over input errors. In both tests, the photographer was also instructed to take the photos when the subject's face was "at rest." Even "at rest" can have more than one meaning when exact measurements are to be taken. But where the data is the result of opinion and is relative, rather than dimensional, minor variation of facial features, such as tension and fatigue, has slight effect on the input accuracy. The viewer usually "reads through" such emotions.

It is hoped that further work will be done on computerized files of facial features for identification. Faces are as different as fingerprints, and every seeing human being is skilled in recognizing faces. Standards must be acquired and fixed routines established to make facial identification reliable.

GRAPHIC AIDS TO FACIAL IDENTIFICATION

Many large police departments have sketch artists whose skill is to make line sketches from the descriptions given by witnesses. Their skill is as much psychological as it is artistic, as they question people for details of a suspect's face. They must also have infinite patience and much experience. In working with someone practiced in identification methods who had a good chance to see the suspect, such as a bank teller or immigration officer, an hour may produce a sketch of amazing likeness. With victims of violent crimes, the artist may have to work many hours, spread over a period of days, to finish his sketch. The next step usually, is to send this picture out to all police organizations. The sketch may also be released in the newspapers and on TV, with the public being asked to watch out for the criminal. Again, it is noted that everyone is an expert at facial recognition.

There are new methods for smaller departments, and some police chiefs feel these new methods are even better than the artist approach. In these, the victim (or witness) is shown a photo or sketch exhibiting only one feature, perhaps the hair or only the eyes in making his description. But he has the choice of many types of eyes, each pair on a separate transparency showing eyes only. From this series of sketches or photos, a composition is made. Often, this method, too, produces a striking resemblance.

The best known of these composite methods is the Identi-Kit®, produced in Irvine, California. Developed by a Los Angeles police officer in 1958,[7] the method has been commercially available to police departments for nearly twenty years. There are now over 3,000 kits in use throughout the world. Two models are now available: One uses photographs and the other, sketches. Both use the same principle of overlaying transparencies.

The kit consists of over five hundred transparencies, called *foils*. Each is a graphic representation of a distinguishing feature of a person's face.[8] For example, there are over one hundred hair types, each pictured alone on a transparency. The witness, aided by someone trained in the method, selects the one that seems to fit the suspect best. Next, a pair of eyes are chosen from over a hundred foils and placed beneath the hair. Then eyebrows are selected, then nose, and so on until the face is complete. Because each sheet is transparent, except for its one feature picture, superimposing a dozen or so in a stack creates an entire face. The eyes can be raised or lowered, as can the hairline or any other feature, to improve the likeness. The assembled picture is then photographed for release to the media.

Each foil is coded with a number, so to send a copy to other police areas where a similar kit is available, only the numbers are sent by teleprinter or verbally over the telephone. The system has an excellent record as an aid in forensic identification.

For use in access control or transaction, it seems the system has little to offer. It is slow and requires training and experience on the part of the user. There may be some use, however, in the numbers generated. Is it possible to type individuals by their face, as well as their fingerprint? The system lends itself to 62 billion combinations, but the typical individual can be described in 16 three-digit numbers. This means a person's face could be digitized and stored in a fraction of the computer storage required for his monthly bank statement. Certainly, it would be possible to store the 500 foils on video tape and to generate the composite on a TV screen. A person's face could be put on the magnetic stripe of a credit card, using this system. With the technologies available today, the Identi-Kit does not have to be foils and decimal numbers.

FACIAL IDENTIFICATION AS A METHOD

The technologies employed in the facial ID field are totally outnumbered by the everyday human effort at facial recognition. There have been less than a dozen projects in the field. Yet, there seems to be a natural interpersonal difference in faces that can be of value. The field needs more work and more experts if it is to take its place as a respected means of automated personal identification.

REFERENCES

1. Harmon, L. D. and Hunt, W. F.: Automatic recognition of human face profiles. *Computer Graphics and Image Processing.* New York, Acad Pr, 1977.
2. Meldelson, F. F.: The great (photo identification) card game. *Security Management, 21(1):* 1977.
3. Van Emden, B.: *A Check List for Photo Identification Security.* Read before the Input-Output Systems Seminar, New York, 1974.
4. Mayer, G. L.: Personal communication with the author, Jan., 1977.
5. Harmon, L. D.: The recognition of faces. *Sci Am, 229(5):* 1973.
6. Harmon, L. D., Kuo, S. C., Ramig, P. F., and Raudkivi, J.: *Identification of Human Face Profiles by Computer.* First-year report to Air Force, 1976. (Under contract AF-30602-75-C-0121); *Image Processing,* in press.
7. Sondern, F.: The box that catches criminals. *Reader's Digest, 84(504):* 1964.
8. Identi-kit continues to score. *Fingerprint and Identification, 55(1):* 1973.

Chapter 11

CONCLUSION

In the previous ten chapters, identification has been reviewed from all aspects. The history, the place of ID in today's world, and the impact on modern society were all discussed in regard to personal identification as a function. Chapter 4, then, dealt with fundamentals of the method and how it applied to automated or machine-aided identification.

The remaining chapters treated individual methods, voice, fingerprints, passwords, and the technologies (usually computers) that support them. As with any technology, it is in constant change. Computer technology is perhaps changing more rapidly than any other field of science, as are current identification methods, since they are dominantly computer oriented.

FUTURE TECHNOLOGIES

It is difficult and risky to forecast the future of any technology. The advances of the past two decades particularly make one wary of guessing the future. The advent of mechanical power, to replace animal power in the nineteenth century, caused a massive upheaval in the everyday lives of the entire civilized world. Yet, the average man could grasp the change, and the sociologists and the philosophers understood and could visualize mechanical motion. The workings of muscles and mechanical levers were not only similar, but they were visible and tangible.

The computer and its offspring are replacing mental activity, which is a field man does not understand. Scanners and microphones are replacing sensory organs, whose functions are accepted but inexplicable. Magnetic memories, which never fail and make human brains look shamefully error prone, are replacing what used to be memorized or written down.

Even though the human brain is vastly more capable than even the smartest of today's computers, the gap is bound to narrow as computers are improved, because the capability of the brain

181

is not improving as generations come into being. True, we seem "smarter" than the society of 1,000 years ago, but we are the same assembly of flesh, blood, and soul. We are not really any more intellectually capable than our forebearers, merely better informed and better equipped.

Since identification is an intellectual, rather than a physical accomplishment, its future is closely tied to the computer and the artificial intelligence machines. Yet, identification requires that these devices take their data from the human being. Unlike the computer, which works with other computers or deals in numbers, the ID computer must deal with man. Today, most computerized ID is performed by supplying the identifyee with something the computer can understand, i.e. a card or a memorized password. A few systems operate on natural attributes, such as voice or fingerprints, but even in these, the information is extracted by requiring the identifyee to perform an act.

Tomorrow's identification systems will not require that the identifyee participate in the act. His mere presence will supply enough data for a sensor a few feet away to identify him. It may be by smell, aura, or some radiated field as yet unknown, or by a summary of unchangeable physical characteristics. Probably, the presence of three or more people will confuse the sensor, and the identifyee will have to isolate himself during the act of identification. However, if the ID device is in the hands of an operator, it will probably be capable of focus, so that the proper person can be selected out of a group. No doubt police will have ID devices like rifles, that can be pointed at one person in a crowd and extract the personal data for later analysis. The currently prevalent technique of verification will have been replaced by direct identification.

I expect that before any technology reaches this point, there would be some attempt to implant an identification module in each person at birth. To those of us in a free state, this is anathema. But to the many millions who live under totalitarian rule and who have to present credentials countless numbers of times each day, such a system would be a relief.[1] Today, in the United States, the Social Security number is issued at the time we become adult and follows us to the grave. We each use it hundreds of times. It was once suggested that this number be indelibly marked on each of us at birth, thus, it would be available as a means of ID. Fortunately, this was roundly rejected by the government.

Any system or any technology has flaws, and no doubt, in each step toward a universal identification system, there will be occasional failures. The courts will be full, as they are today, of cases proving who did a certain act. There will be counterfeit rings who alter IDs so that the sensors make mistakes. There will be ways to mask the sensors and make them inoperative or permanently disable them. But I believe that, in the end, there will be good means of positive identification without the identifyee overtly participating. To some, it will be distasteful, to some even unacceptable, but in a generation or two, these minorities will dwindle.

Why should one resist being identified? Of course, if you are doing a wrong, you would not want to be identified and made to pay for it. But that is what most ID is for—to keep people from wrong doing. The person living a normal life, even though competitive, should not resist identifying himself. To be known and recognized is not an invasion of privacy.[2] The urban life of today brings us in such close contact that the so-called right to privacy is at once more meaningful, yet less attainable. We must learn to respect our neighbor's sphere—and stay out of it, even at some considerable effort. In turn, he will stay out of ours. Once there is intrusion, however, there must be recourse to the courts, and this means the parties must be identified.

Before a universal identifier is available, even before serious thought is given to implanting a device at birth, some interim solutions must be available. Already, industrial plants need to protect their property and their corporate secrets. Shared-computer nets must assure their users that the data is safe, and business transactions must be secure. To achieve this in today's technology (and with today's public) each area must be treated differently.

At plant entry, the currently popular photo card will, no doubt, continue to do the job. The guards may be aided by video files and closed TV circuits and, perhaps, machine-aided ID. It will be five to twelve years, however, before computer ID of faces is an economic reality. By then, automated fingerprint or voice analysis may be existent.

For shared nets, the password will continue. A password is not personal identification–but considering the physical security surrounding the terminals in shared nets, the password is adequate. The memorized images of the I.D. Code System seem exceptionally well-suited to identifying a party in a shared net.

In business transactions involving the public, signature dynamics will undoubtedly become the accepted method. It is cheap, it is secret, and the public is already used to a signature. As yet, no workable system is available, and certainly it could be killed by a clumsily wired pen or the restriction of rigid forms design–but these are not necessary. Properly engineered, signature dynamics will usher in a new acceptance of identification at the point of transaction. Until such a system comes on the market, the PIN number will have to serve.

The first big change–and it has already started–is in wholesale banking. This business has had passwords and encryption for fifty years and is now computerizing the entire concept. In this field, the originator (password), the text (encrypted), and the exact amount (protected by check digits) is all composed and transmitted in milliseconds by a computer. These systems are not experimental; they are in everyday use.

This is the beginning, and all too soon, perhaps by the year 2000, all business and most of our personal lives will be conducted in an environment where we are known and where we know we are known, even though we are in an unfamiliar area. To pretend and assume a false identity will be economically unfeasible. Today, it is merely illegal and often profitable. Perhaps, then, honesty will no longer be the virtue of a few–it will be forced upon everyone.

REFERENCES

1. National identity cards: A way to fight fraud? *U.S. News and World Report, 79(11):* 1975.
2. Baxter, W. F., Cootner, P. H., and Scott, K. E.: *Retail Banking in the Electronic Age.* Montclair, New Jersey, Allenhead, 1977.

INDEX

185